Advance Reviews for

Watching the Hand of the Lord

I can bear personal witness to the exercise of faith manifest in this book. Whether blessing or heartache, the center of family life is Christ Jesus, and Christ is manifest also in the children in faith and service. The author captures the essence of Joel 1:2–3, "Hear this, ye old men, and give ear, all ye inhabitants of the land. Hath this been in your days, or even in the days of your fathers? Tell ye your children of it, and let your children tell their children, and their children another generation."

Jackie's book is a book of the record of God's direction and guidance in the journey of life. Most of all, it is a testimony to the abundant grace of God, Who calls and strengthens His children as they journey through the different avenues of life, the joys and vicissitudes of life, toward their heavenly home. Thank You, Lord.

Daniel Fleischer
Pastor Emeritus, Church of the Lutheran Confession (CLC)

In this heartfelt memoir that spans the recent century, Jackie Radichel traces the imprints of God's grace throughout the history of her family. Her impressive memory and genuine voice make the story of how Jackie met her husband Phil a compelling read, from how the Lord prepared them for each other through Christian parents and grandparents, to how He brought them together, and how He blessed them with the gift of their four children and ten grandchildren. Readers will find themselves caught up in the lives of the Radichel and Sandeen families, as well as delighted by fascinating historical details and events woven throughout. This book is for anyone who enjoys seeing how God is faithful to His people across the ages and how He keeps His promises to those who trust in Him. As Jackie herself states over and over in her book, "Thank You, Lord!"

Debra Mayhew
Editor, *The Branches* magazine

Lard sandwiches. Broken noses. Lives blessed with wise counsel and guided by God's Word. Jackie Radichel's earnest recounting of her family's history—part genealogy, part time capsule, part Christian testimony—covers four generations of family lore and details the sweet legacy of shared faith. By connecting life experiences with relevant scriptural references and original verse, Jackie has constructed a personal history that is relatable to both friends and relations. But this retelling also speaks to a broader audience: those who enjoy sampling snippets of recent history, those who seek nourishment for the soul, and those who will appreciate the dedication to biblical values that is apparent throughout. God's love-light shines through this interesting and accomplished family, and that is encouragement to us all.

Sue Anne Kirkham
Author, *Loving Zelda: A Stepdaughter's Caregiving Journal*

Jackie Radichel's book, *Watching the Hand of the Lord*, is the story of her faith-life journey. This book will bless her children, grandchildren, great-grandchildren, and friends who have shared some of these experiences. But it also will benefit a larger audience and remind all of us how the hand of the Lord is always guiding us in all our ways. The book of Hebrews in chapter 12 reminds the children of God that we are surrounded by so great a cloud of witnesses. Jackie's book remembers the cloud of witnesses that surrounded her and enabled her to run with endurance the race that God set before her. Her life story reminds us to look to Jesus, the founder and perfecter of our faith. Or as she emphasizes, "But seek first the kingdom of God and his righteousness and all these (other) things will be added to you" (ESV).

John Schierenbeck
Pastor Emeritus, Church of the Lutheran Confession (CLC)

Watching
THE HAND OF
the Lord

Jacquelyn G. (Sandeen) Radichel

ERBEN HOUSE

To the memory of our parents,

for the examples they set for us and

whose lives were based on faith in God and prayer

to His throne for their daily strength and guidance

To our children,

whose souls by God's grace were given to us

To our grandchildren,

who will need to "mark and avoid" the false

doctrine that will work its way into the church

www.erbenhouse.com

Photo credits: All photos are from the Jacquelyn Radichel personal archive, either given to, purchased by, or created by the author.
Cover design by Tim Schaser.
Interior design by Tina Eichstadt and Sarah J. Olmanson.

ISBN 979-8-9865934-0-1

Printed in the United States of America
First printing

Contents

Foreword

"One day at a time—that's the only way
the good Lord gives it to us."

If there were ever a classic quote from my mother in her later years, this statement would be near the top. She means it in an all-encompassing way, across any foreseeable topic. Certainly, it undergirds her perspective on life in general, and therefore across the pages you are about to read. It also illustrates how books are written—one day at a time.

As I reflect on the years of conversations about why Mom chose to document her memories in this way, her unwavering goal remained consistent—a documentation of God's ever-present hand in her own life and the lives of those around her for the blessing and remembrance of future generations. My mind leaps immediately to Deuteronomy chapter six.

> And these words that I command you today shall be on your heart. You shall teach them diligently to your children, and shall talk of them when you sit in your house, and when you walk by the way, and when you lie down, and when you rise. You shall bind them as a sign on your hand, and they shall be as frontlets between your eyes. You shall write them on the doorposts of your house and on your gates (ESV).

Personal memoirs are relatively common in publishing. We all have a story to tell. Yet even with the vast number of personal stories that are committed to print, fewer are published if for no other reason than some grit is required to finish a work. This book has been roughly twenty years in writing and decades more in the making and learning.

Parents grant yet another gift to their children and others around them when they accomplish a life-long goal—the gift of seeing tangible fruits from an extended labor with long-delayed gratification. In our evermore instantaneous world, this example rings true as a gift and a lesson.

Something sets this work apart from others, however. At times you sense that a storyteller lacks clarity on the meaning across life events. Perhaps the author chooses to withhold conclusions or lessons throughout the unfolding narrative. The highs and lows of life, tumultuous or otherwise, simply create an engaging read or some unique set of noteworthy events. In the end, you often are left to draw your own conclusions, or you must wait for the "what does this all mean," which comes at the end.

This book is different. It's less musing, wondering, and discovering, and more evidence-based reporting. Not reporting like an article in the newspaper might be, but personal and direct in its conclusion/conviction and theme from the very first page. There is no questioning in this story, no building to a conclusion or awareness like an inductive argument. It is the opposite—thesis first, evidence-building second.

What's the big deal about that? Well, for this book, it could be written in no other way. A clear, confident voice of truth speaks from a soul bonded to her Creator by the Spirit's saving faith-gift in Jesus Christ. Mom wanted to write down her stories so they could be remembered down through the generations, yes; but what she really writes is a testimony to her faith and God's omniscience as Keeper of all things large and small—each day, every day.

We all bring multiple perspectives to a book. For me, it's as a fellow child of God, first and foremost. Daughter, wife, mother, friend. Avid reader across genres. From this personal side, part of Mom's book is my own life, of course; the rest of it covers people I love deeply. A personal perspective reminds me of my own history and my future in heaven—a timeless timeline of God's grace. Yes, I can vouch for many of the details, whether directly or indirectly, and this volume will be an important and respected piece of our family's history.

From a professional perspective, I work as a speech-language pathologist with more than twenty-five years in the publishing industry. One of the daily roles that I enjoy involves working directly with authors, so as I read Mom's book, I reflect on the journey that authors must go through every time they craft a work. Partnering with authors to produce something that is most meaningful to them is always a privilege and often a dance. Supporting this work has been no different. I don't usually high-five my authors, but I would with this one!

What delights me is not only that Mom told her story, but also that she finished it just as she wanted. What you are about to read is one woman's perspective on God's hand through the generations surrounding and including her life. But it's not just about her, she will tell you quickly. In some ways, the story is ubiquitous because each of us has many similar life details. In Mom's life and writing, we can all see ourselves, but more importantly we can see the hand of the Lord.

I won't forget the hours I sat next to Mom at her computer—the emphatic statements she would make about the "Why?" of a particular event. The intensity of wanting to "get the story right." The incredulity when I asked a probing question that didn't matter—". . .because that's the way God chose to do it, Tina!" That's seventy-seven years of a brilliant child-like faith and more than a little gumption to dismiss the psychobabble that tempts us. It is, perhaps, the adult version of "God said it, I believe it, that settles it." Refreshingly simple, isn't it?

As you read this book, hear the stories, but listen to the message. It is your message too—the hand of the Lord guides and keeps us all.

Tina (Radichel) Eichstadt
March 2022

Introduction

What keeps families together? FAITH.

Over the past 20 years or so I have been working on writing my life story. I have discussed many aspects of this with family members and friends from church and in my daily life who have continually encouraged me along the way. The reason I decided to write my story in the first place and make it into a book was to pass on what I learned from early on in life not only to my children and my children's children, but to encourage others to "*seek first*" (Matthew 6:33) God's Word and to know that He is always with you. "*Pray without ceasing*" (I Thessalonians 5:17) as you watch the hand of the Lord daily in all you do and experience in life.

Several perspectives led me to want to write this book:

First, as I looked back on how I grew up and what happened in my life while learning about the Lord, and how my husband grew up and how he learned about the Lord, these memories made a big impact on how I lived my life. And as I watched the hand of the Lord in my life, I saw the great importance of childhood instruction for myself and for our children as we applied God's Word to our daily lives.

Second, parenting is one thing; grandparenting is another. If you've taught your children about the Lord, in how and why you raised them as you did, you can pray that they will teach their children likewise. Therefore, continue to pray and encourage the parents while also encouraging the grandchildren to listen to their parents and the Lord. I want my grandchildren to discern the difference between what the Lord teaches in His Word and what the world inserts into, or deletes from, Scripture. We all need to watch out for the worldly deceptions that Satan injects into everyday living. It's so important to remind the younger generation that they are God's special people—"*a chosen generation*" (1 Peter 2:9).

Third, I'm not here to open closets and let out the skeletons of my life, but to show how God helps us move past the skeletons and leads us to where we need to be for His plan. We all have our skeletons! Instead, walk with me and watch His hand at work in my life as I trace the steps that brought two individuals together to do the work He had for us to do. You too may be able to see His hand at work in your life.

Finally, may you be certain of His grace and abide in His truth knowing that "*all things work together for good to them that love God, to them who are the called according to His purpose*" (Romans 8:28). And then hear Him say, "*Be still, and know that I am God*" (Psalm 46:10) and that He is "*with you always, even unto the end of the world. Amen*" (Matthew 28:20).

TO GOD BE THE GLORY

Chapter I

Our Parents

The fear of the LORD is the beginning of wisdom
and the knowledge of the holy is understanding.

Proverbs 9:10

Everything starts somewhere and everything starts with God. Retrospect is looking back. Even though my husband claims "You can't go back!" I believe children can benefit from knowing how their parents grew up. In this way each one of us can see why we are who we are and especially to see how God has shaped each of us as His child to do what He has for us to do during the time of grace He gives each of us to have on the earth.

Life is somewhat about heritage—where we came from, the genes and the backgrounds, how one grew up, the circumstances, the basics that formed who we are, and the legacy developed for those who come after us. And yet our legacy is not about us, it is all about God.

As we open our eyes to the wonders of God, we find He is always near and working for our good. It is watching a journey through life where we see the unseen blessings mature to allow us eventually to see His real blessings and give Him thanks for them.

For many years I have desired to leave a written legacy for our children and grandchildren that told the story about my husband and me—where we each came from, our growing up years (i.e., our heritage), how we met, and where the Lord took us from there. The older I have become, the more intense my desire has been to complete this story.

> Oh, that the Lord would guide my way
> To keep His statutes still!
> Oh, that my God would grant me grace
> To know and do His will!
>
> Author: Isaac Watts, Text: Public Domain

On Thursday, October 7, 1943, in Albert Lea, Minnesota, a baby boy was born to Gilbert Raymond and Valborg Amanda (nee Levorson) Radichel. They named him Philip Edwin.

On Tuesday, February 13, 1945, in Sioux City, Iowa, a baby girl was born to Charles Henry and Rosa Anna Elsie (nee Schmidt) Sandeen. They named her Jacquelyn Gerane.

In God's way and in His timing these two young people met in June 1960, on the steps of Our Redeemer's Lutheran Church in Red Wing, Minnesota. Their journey to that place at that moment in time and where their lives took them after that was continually blessed by the Lord.

It all starts with love—God's love for us. For, *"God is love"* (1 John 4:8) and *"God so loved the world, that He gave His only begotten Son, that whosoever believeth in Him should not perish, but have everlasting life"* (John 3:16). As we look back on our lives, surely it is God who shaped us through our parents. And so it goes on from generation to generation.

> *We will not hide them* [sayings of old] *from their children,*
> *shewing to the generation to come the praises of the LORD, and*

his strength, and his wonderful works that he hath done.

Psalm 78:4

My Mother

Rosa Anna Elsie Schmidt, my mother, was born Sunday, March 3, 1918, in Watertown, South Dakota. Her parents, Otto Reinhardt and Genevieve Marie (nee Gallisath) Schmidt, had her baptized shortly thereafter. At some point in Mom's first ten years, her family moved to Sioux City. She was the middle child of seven children: John, Earl, Margaret, Rosey, Mildred, Dorothy, and Shirley. They mostly called her Rosey when she was younger. Later, she was called Ann. At one point she legally had her name on her driver's license as R Ann Sandeen. Over the years of their marriage, I know many people called her Sandy as well.

Grandpa Otto, my mother's father, worked at several different places, but I know at one point he worked for the railroad. It was during that time in 1941 that he got caught between the train cars when the train lurched ahead, rolling over Grandpa's leg. His leg was damaged so severely that the doctor amputated it about six inches below the knee and fitted him with an artificial foot and leg. Even as a young child, I remember seeing his leg standing in the room when he wasn't wearing it. It was made of some kind of lightweight fiberglass-like material and had half-inch holes in it to allow air to circulate through to his stump. He had

My Mom
High School Graduation (1936)

to wear a wool stocking on the stump to keep it from being rubbed raw when he walked.

I was always Grandpa Otto's fishing buddy when he came to Minnesota. Mom would tell me to keep an eye on Grandpa because if he fell into the water, the water would fill up his hollow leg and pull him under. She must have thought I would be able to do something about it to save him!

I never knew my mother's mother, Genevieve. They called her Jenny Marie. When her last child, Shirley Jean, was born on Tuesday, January 14, 1936, Jenny became ill and remained hospitalized for some time. When she did get to go home, she was still very sick. My mother, eighteen years old at this time, had spruced up her mom's room and even made new curtains for it. When Jenny arrived home, Mom asked her how she liked the room and the curtains, but Jenny couldn't even see them. By this time her illness had made her blind. Whenever Mom would relive those days, her comments reflected her disappointment that her mother never got to see what she had worked on so hard for her. Jenny died shortly after coming home.

Imagine seven children—the youngest only months old—with four still at home and no mother to keep the household running smoothly. The oldest three siblings were married so my mother seemed to be the one designated to cook, clean, sew, and help take care of Shirley. Mom was a senior in high school at the time and worked at a bakery to help with expenses at home. She was fortunate to be able to bring home leftover bread that would have been thrown out otherwise. The cost of bread at that time, Mom said, was ten cents a loaf.

Some of the meals Mom remembered having as a child in the 1920s were lard sandwiches or tapioca pudding which her mother fixed for the family. Mom said there would be a large bowl, the kind used for making bread, filled with tapioca pudding in the middle of the table. Everyone got a spoon and when the pudding was gone, you were done. That was their meal! The same happened when they had the lard sandwiches. It's no wonder most of them died later of heart disease, even though they were very skinny! I'm sure all the smoking that they did as teenagers and beyond added to that problem. I know I still have a big smoke allergy having grown up in a household of two 2-pack-a-day smokers.

Growing up in the depression era, Mom learned all about "waste not, want not" and recycled everything long before recycling was fashionable. When she cooked for us, if food was left over, we ate it the next day, or the next, until it was either gone or moldy. If it was moldy, it went into the compost heap for the garden, along with coffee grounds and vegetable peelings. If it was clothes that we had outgrown, she handed them down to other kids less fortunate, even though we had already gotten them from our cousins.

After Mom and Dad were married on May 1, 1938, Mom continued her working pace as we moved from Somerset, Wisconsin to Ellsworth, Wisconsin to Hay Creek, Minnesota and on to places in Red Wing—215 College Avenue, 1224 Phelps Street, 206 E 5th Street. Finally, in 1953, Dad and Mom bought *Sandy Acres* on Twin Bluff Road (Route 4), just outside the Red Wing city limits. This was the first house they owned, the others all having been rented. So, for the small sum of $4,400 they bought five acres with a two-story house that had been built near a creek fifty years earlier and had been moved several miles up the hill to a new foundation on this property. They purchased this property with the house that had no kitchen cupboards, no kitchen floors—just studs to walk on—no water in the house, BUT boasted new white metal cupboards still boxed in the basement and had a new installed furnace. The house had four bedrooms on the upper floor along with a large L-shaped living room, dining room, kitchen area, and future bathroom on the main floor. The house footprint was 24' x 24' with a lot of hard work ahead.

First House, Sandy Acres Fix-up (1953)

Mom used to say, "If you buy something, buy the best so it will last." In 1954, she bought a gray sectional for the living room. It had three pieces: a 2-piece loveseat that could be used together with an arm on the opposite end of each piece and a 1-piece section half that size with no arms on it. You could arrange it in many ways. Mom would even wrap a corner wall with it. She loved it and it worked well in our home. I know she paid a lot of money for it and had worked hard to pay it off.

Eleven years later, when I was engaged, Mom spent the same amount of money again to buy heavy duty gold fabric to have that sectional reupholstered. After our wedding in 1966, she always kept it covered with a sheet so it wouldn't get dirty. Twenty years later, after Dad died and we moved Mom to the Twin Cities, she still would not take the sheets off it except when company came. Finally, after Mom died in 1994, we brought that gold couch to our home and

Mom bought the best, it stood the test! (1954)

never put the sheets on it again! More than sixty years from when it was originally purchased, that couch still served a purpose in our family room. Grandchildren were allowed to sit on it, and it still was as clean looking as the day Mom bought it. I couldn't even give it away to our children—they were tired of seeing it. When my brother, Jim, and his wife, Carol, moved to Eau Claire, Wisconsin, I gave it to them. They use it in their family room—without sheets—and it still looks new!

Mother worked hard outside the home as far back as I can remember. She did secretarial work at Weiman's radio and TV repair business and then my dad's radio and TV repair business in the early 1950s in Red Wing. She also painted dishes at the famous Red Wing Pottery in the late 1950s, hung hoses for the Durkee Atwood Company, and did sewing at the Knitting Mills. After that, she had various shoe factory jobs at LaGrange Shoe Company and finally Riedell Shoe Company. She retired from Riedell's in 1978. She always worked hard! Mom was an excellent and appreciated employee; wherever she worked, she was dependable, on time, and gave 100%.

One of the major things I learned from my mother from early on was her love of her Lord and Savior. From an infant my parents brought music to me in song and dance. Mother always sang as she rocked me to sleep. "Jesus Loves Me" was the first song I remember her singing. She loved to sing and sang in the church choir as long as she could. She had a big voice that carried.

I remember when I was five years old, Dad used to get up on Sunday morning and take us to church and Sunday School. He would drop us off and return home to bed. Later he would get up, eat breakfast, and come back to church to pick us up again. I remember asking Mom why Daddy didn't come to church with us. She told me to "just keep praying and some day he will." I never forgot that; however, I remember *always* praying that the Lord would give me a man of my own faith who would always go to church with me.

Another example of how Mom lived her faith, and there were many, occurred when she worked at Riedell Shoe Company. A man on a cutting machine in front of her machine would swear a lot and use the name of the Lord in vain when things went wrong. It got to the point where Mother couldn't stand it anymore, and when he would say "Jesus Christ" in a loud voice, she would simply say, *"the same yesterday, and today, and forever"* (Hebrews 13:8). After a while, the man quit using that phrase at work! Thank You, Lord, for the Christian example of my mother.

I learned many things from, or because of, my mother over the years. She always was a very spiritual woman, but emotionally insecure. Her dominance came from lack of self-esteem. My husband once said, "She always tried to do things for people, whether they wanted her to or not." And even though she really did mean well by it, and it was a fruit of her faith, her flesh got in the way at times and occasionally she wouldn't let them forget what she did for them. As I went through my childhood, and then through high school, I also developed what is often called an inferiority complex. I was always trying to do as much as I could to get approval of my parents, teachers, and even my friends. It took many years until my husband finally straightened me out. Along the way I developed the joy of helping others, as I'm sure Mom also felt, *without* needing anything in return. Thank You, Lord, for a mother that taught me many things, in many ways, but always through her love for You, her Lord and Savior.

My Father

Charles Henry Sandeen, my father, was born on Friday, December 6, 1912, in Sioux City, to Henning August and Lillian Jo (nee Woolridge) Sandeen. He was the first child of two. I was told by my father and my grandmother that my great-grandparents came over from Sweden. They also told me that their name had been Erickson when they came to this country, but because there were so many Ericksons—more than seventy according to my brother, Jim—in the community of Peoria, Illinois, where they settled, they changed the name to Sandeen. I haven't been able to confirm that, but I will take it as family information. From my perspective of what I've heard, Henning was an intelligent man and worked as a bank teller, always striving to provide for his wife and their two children—my dad, Charles, and his sister, Doris Gerane, who was born Saturday, June 14, 1919.

My Dad
High School Graduation
(1930)

Dad's mother, Lillian, was a librarian. In trying to meet his family's needs, Henning used his skills of accounting to "borrow" from bank funds. After some time, the bank examiners found out about his "personal loans" and sent him to prison. He told my dad once, "It takes a smart man to keep a set of books, but it takes a **** sight smarter man to keep a set of crooked books." Somewhere in the time frame after Henning was sent to prison, Dad's mother, Lillian, took his sister, Gerane, and moved to Kansas City, Kansas, where Lillian could find work. Grandma Lil used to tell me stories about those hard times when there wasn't enough money to heat their apartment. She and Gerane, a small child at the time, would sleep together so their bodies could provide the heat to get through the night. All this time Henning remained in prison. Meanwhile, at about the age of eight, my dad was sent to live with his Uncle Ranny (Randall) and Auntie Gladdy (Gladys) Van Houten on a farm near Correctionville, Iowa. In his teen years, he not only did the farm work, but also drove the horse-drawn milk wagon to make deliveries.

In Correctionville High School, Dad played on the football team and played trumpet in the band. Like his father, he was also very intelligent and worked for a bank, although I'm not sure if it was the same bank where his father worked. I do know that the bank president would have paid to have Dad go to college, but Dad turned it down to marry his high school sweetheart, Velma Monk. They married in 1930 when they graduated. They had two children: Doris Ellen (born Wednesday, May 25, 1932) and Charles Henry Jr. (born Sunday, August 13, 1933). Although Dad and Velma were divorced in 1936, and Dad married Mom in 1938, there was at least some connection between Dad and Mom and Doris and Charlie in the years that followed.

I talked to Doris a couple of weeks before she died on Thursday, July 21, 2011. I asked her what her memories were of her parents, Dad and Velma. She said that Velma, her mother, was born on Monday, May 29, 1911, and was a schoolteacher. They lived in Correctionville at the time. Doris thought that Grandma Lil probably had something to do with Dad and Velma's divorce. Doris said she was four at the time and didn't really remember much.

Over the years, I remember how Mom always tried to keep the connection going between Dad and his children. Mom always sent gifts to them from Dad for birthdays and Christmas. Still, Doris said she and Charlie were bitter toward Dad because he wouldn't come to see them. Doris said when she was about ten in 1942, Velma even brought the kids to see Dad who was working for the government in Sioux City, in the Office of Price Administration (OPA). Doris also remembered when my dad and mom lived in an

Dad *(circled)* married his high school classmate Velma Monk (1930) *(circled)*

apartment in Sioux City. On one Christmas, she and Charlie slept on a cot in their living room. Mom brought in toys for them for Christmas Eve. Velma's side of the family gave Mom a hard time, and Mom cried because she was just trying to help. Doris's daughter, Linda, told me she had no memory of Dad, only of my mom as "sweet Grandma Ann." My mother cared for people, more than a lot of people early on in her life really understood. It even took me many years to see her love in what she did for me, but her heart belonged to Jesus.

By their fruits ye shall know them.
Matthew 7:20

Dad and Mom met through Mom's brother, Earl Schmidt, lovingly called "Schmitty." I don't remember how Dad and Earl met, but I do know that Earl introduced Mom to Dad at a dance. As I heard the story, Mom came to the dance with another guy and went home from the dance with Dad. I'm not sure about all of the timing, but it wasn't long until Mom and Dad ran away to Vermillion, South Dakota, to get married by the justice of the peace on Sunday, May 1, 1938. Their friends, Ben and Vadna Shelton, went with them as witnesses. They didn't tell anyone for several weeks. Finally, Mom said to her dad that they were married. Otto asked how long they had been married. When Mom told him "a couple of weeks," Otto laughed—he thought it had been longer than that! When will children learn they can't fool their parents? As a side note, Mom had handmade/knitted her wedding dress. That must have taken some time for her to do. Still, she was ready when they ran away to get married. She did love to sew, and I always had new dresses for the holidays or special occasions.

Uncle Earl, Mom's brother, was a Sioux City policeman (joined in 1942) and retired as a detective sergeant in 1968. During those years, he was responsible for several brave acts as a policeman. I remember hearing about two of them most of all. When the Floyd River flooded in 1953, Uncle Earl got people out of a grocery store through the roof as the water rose in the building. They had to be rescued by boat, but he had been the one to take them to safety initially.

Another event that Uncle Earl was known for was the February 1960 shooting of Jack Delaney, one of the ten most wanted men in America at one time, reportedly! Uncle Earl was a top marksman pistol shooter and was the first officer to arrive on the call to the Sunshine grocery store where a robbery was in progress. He got there after two masked robbers had gone into the store. One of the robbers was corralling store employees and customers into a store cooler in the back of the store while Delaney was robbing the till. When he saw Uncle Earl coming in, he started firing his gun. Uncle Earl took cover behind a support post and shot several times as the robber kept coming toward him shooting. It took several shots, one directly to his heart, to finally drop him. J. Edgar Hoover, the FBI director at the time, sent Earl a commendation for his brave act.

After Dad and Mom moved to *Sandy Acres* on Twin Bluff Road in 1953, I remember Charlie, Dad's son, came to stay with us for a summer. Work had been hard to find in Iowa and Charlie got a job at the Rock Wool plant by Frontenac, a community a few miles south of Red Wing. Mom required Charlie to pay rent, because she cooked for him and washed his clothes. I don't think Charlie liked that idea much, but paid it weekly. At the end of the summer, when Charlie was packed, in the car, and ready to drive away, I watched Mom hand him an envelope that contained everything he had paid to her. Her comment to his surprised face was, "You need to learn that you have to pay your way in this world." With that, he drove away.

Those words came back to me years later when I was in college, paying my own way, and went home to ask for $500 to help with tuition that year. The answer was, "No, we can't afford it." Although I was frustrated with the answer, I should have known from Charlie's experience what I would hear. In my young adult mind, I started selfishly to compare what my parents had given me with what they had given my brother—private schooling and seminary training, among other things—and it didn't seem fair. Now, having parented four children of our own, I realize that parents often *wisely* make decisions not based on equality among children, but based on differing gifts and needs. As I have matured in self-discipline, as well as in years, I so appreciate watching the hand of the Lord and how He taught me His ways through my parents while I was growing up.

My son, hear the instruction of thy father,
and forsake not the law of thy mother.
Proverbs 1:8

My daddy was a special kind of man—gentle, loyal, warm, and friendly, and always with a twinkle in his eye. I was always "Daddy's Little Girl." He would often sing the song with the same title to me, mostly out of the blue when he would just look at me across the table or if we were riding together in the car as he was taking me some place. He would sing, "You're the spirit of Christmas, my star on the tree. You're the Easter bunny to Mommy and me. You're sugar, you're spice, you're everything nice, and you're Daddy's little girl." I also loved his endearing mellow voice singing "You Are My Sunshine" as his baby blue eyes sparkled and twinkled at my delight. When Daddy bought himself a Hammond organ for our house, he took lessons to learn to play all the songs with chords. One of the first songs he learned was "Daddy's Little Girl" just so he could sing it and play it at the same time. Oh, how I loved to hear those words. I really loved Daddy! Thank You, Lord, for bringing him to faith through the Holy Ghost and allowing me to watch Your hand working throughout his life.

Dad and I did special things together. If he was listening to some fun 1940s dance music on the stereo, he would pick me up, when I was younger; or he would grab my hand and pull me off the couch, when I was older, and we would dance to the music all around the living room. He loved music, and he loved to dance! We often would watch TV together—he would sit in his chair, and I would sit on the floor in front of his chair leaning back on him. Long before the Vikings moved to Minnesota, he and I would watch the Packers on the weekends. Yes, I do cheer for the Vikes, but the Packers have a special place in my heart because of my daddy.

My dad had many friends that I remember. He was oftentimes the "life of the party." It was that twinkle in his eye that could always see a funny side of a story or he would have had a smart remark for someone else's story. People always enjoyed being around him.

Dad, like Mom, was a loyal and dependable worker. He always did a great job as he worked at fixing radios and TVs for Ray Weiman in Red Wing. As he began to do his own repair business, he could never get himself to collect back debts from people for the work he did for them. He always figured they really couldn't afford to pay him as the times were hard in the 1940s and 1950s, so he would let the debt accumulate instead of going to collect it. Eventually Mom had to do his bill collecting or we wouldn't have had enough money to pay our bills. Dad liked people and didn't want to push on anyone.

Thy wife shall be as a fruitful vine by the sides of thine house.
Psalm 128:3

During the winter of 1955–56, Dad came home from work one night and began to shave and clean up. Mom loved to tell the story of how she went into the bathroom and asked him where he was going. Dad said to her, "Where do you want me to go?" Somewhat dumbfounded, she turned and walked out of the room. Moments later, she went back in and asked him again, "Where are you going?" Again, he replied, "Where do you want me to go?" Again, she walked out of the room. Finally, as she was hoping beyond hope, she walked in once more and in a soft, pleading, yet knowing voice, she asked the third time, "Where are you going?" A third time he answered, "Where do you want me to go?" By this time, she had figured it out and asked, "Can I come with you?" She realized that he indeed was going to an adult instruction class with Pastor George Barthels regarding the teachings of the Bible. What joy for all of us to watch the changes that came over Dad as, by God's grace, he began to study the Scriptures! Each time Dad came home from a class, you could hear the excitement in his voice as he talked with Mom about what he had learned. Oh, the joy of watching the hand of the Lord working in my father's life.

It happened, as God directed, that my brother, Jim, was being confirmed within the same time frame as Dad's conclusion of his instruction class. Dad had been going to these classes with another friend, Bob Knutson, whose son was also in Jim's class.

So, in the spring of 1956, on the Sunday that the Adult Confirmation Class was to make their personal confession and become members of the church, they all sat in the front row on the right side of the church. As the service began and the Adult Class was ready, Pastor Barthels first asked Dad to come up to the altar area. Much to my amazement, Dad leaned over the baptismal font and was baptized. Being in fifth grade at the time, I was well-aware of the blessings of baptism and the ramifications of not being baptized. I was astonished and horrified to think that my dad had not been baptized before this time. Here was a man of forty-three years who had not been baptized! What if he would have died not being baptized? My mind was thinking all kinds of ill thoughts about my grandmother who had not had my daddy baptized when he was born. So much went through my young mind. I didn't like my grandma much before, but I certainly liked her less that day. How could she, who supposedly was a Christian, not baptize her son, her first born? Her second child, my dear Auntie, had been baptized.

I was thankful to God for giving Mom to Dad, for surely that was God's way of bringing the Gospel to Dad. Mom set the example for Dad and us with her consistent attendance at church and her dedication to seeing that we had a Christian education in our parochial schooling. Thank You, Lord, for this blessing and for her example as we continued to watch the hand of the Lord.

After Dad was baptized, Pastor Barthels then called on the rest of the class to come up to the altar if they were ready to make their confirmation vows. To my added amazement, Bob did not go up for Confirmation but remained seated in the pew—to my knowledge he was never confirmed. I pray that some time before his death years later, he remembered what he had learned and confessed his Savior.

Once Dad was baptized and confirmed, his faithfulness in attending church never wavered and the joy of using his gifts in the work of God's kingdom grew steadily as a fruit of his faith. He always attended services and Bible Class and studied church doctrine. His baptismal service never left me—it had a huge impact on my life. When we had children, we made every effort to have them baptized even before we left the hospital. I could not imagine them not being baptized even for the drive home.

Within a short time after Dad's confirmation there was a major doctrinal difference that had been brewing in the Lutheran churches for some time and finally came to a decision point. Our pastor, along with numerous members including Dad, left their membership in St. John's on Monday, July 22, 1958. Within a week, they organized a new congregation—Our Redeemer's Lutheran Church in Red Wing. My brother, Jim, had been confirmed the same spring as Dad and was now attending high school at Dr. Martin Luther College (DMLC) in New Ulm, Minnesota. I was going into eighth grade in a month but had no parochial school to go to at that point since I had been going to St. John's. It was a major awareness time for me spiritually as I watched the transformation in my father and his deepening spiritual beliefs and his understanding of God's grace to himself, his family, and his church. Watching God's Hand in my dad's life that summer was the single most dramatic moment in my life up to that time.

Within a month, several members of our new little church bought a large two-story house on a bigger piece of property on West Avenue in Red Wing. The house had a former study on the main floor which the congregation turned into a school room. In September of 1958, the school was opened with thirteen students, and I was one of three eighth graders. Two of the teachers that also left St. John's at the same time began as our teachers, but now they had to get outside employment since they could not be paid much by our few members. They worked their employment schedule so one could teach in the morning and one in the afternoon. The Lord continued to bless these two men, Walmar Voigt and Alvin Sieg, and their families to be able to do this service for His Church.

In 1960, when a new church synod, Church of the Lutheran Confession, was organized by like-minded fellow Christians, Dad was privileged to be elected to its first Board of Trustees and served in that position until 1980.

Phil's Mother

As told to me by Phil from his memories of her

Valborg Amanda Levorson was born Saturday, September 28, 1907, in Lake Mills, Iowa. Her parents were Levor Levorson and Ida O. (nee Sagen). Valborg was baptized on Saturday, October 26, 1907, and confirmed on Sunday, June 11, 1922. Valborg was the youngest of fourteen children: Mina Katherine, Lotta, Oscar, Albin Johan, Paul Edwin, Paul Gerhard, Martha Caspara, Herman and Johannes (twins), Nora Henrietta, Ingvald Lauritz, Selmer Adolph, Edwin Leonard, and Valborg Amanda. Levor and Mari Levorson, Valborg and her siblings' grandparents, had come from Norway, settled on land in Iowa, and began to farm the land. The farm was always pretty much self-sufficient and satisfied most of their needs. They originally called it Mariland Farm after Valborg's grandmother, Mari. Her older siblings took care of the farm after their parents died.

Phil's Mom
College Graduation (~1929)

Being the youngest child in the family, Valborg was always the little sister to Mina and Martha, and when Martha said something, Valborg jumped! In the same way, Mina and Martha were always respectful of Selmer, the oldest boy at home at the time, so was her brother, Edwin, for that matter. Selmer wasn't a dictator type, but he was in charge, and everyone knew it! He ran the farm and provided for his brother and sisters because he could, and he did a good job of it. Mina, Martha, Selmer, and Edwin lived on the farm, unmarried, until each one eventually died there. Mina died in the same bed she was born in, ninety-six years later.

Going back in his memory, Phil said he remembered watching Uncle Selmer at work. It was watching somebody with that kind of raw intelligence and capability of doing things without anyone teaching him. He was not taught by his father but was self-taught. Uncle Selmer did see some things that his father did, but his father was almost an invalid by the time Uncle Selmer got to the point where he was running things. Of course, it was a big family and a big farm.

Being in this large farming family meant there was always a lot of work to be done and everyone had to be involved. Since Phil was the oldest boy in his family, he was the one that got to work with Uncle Selmer and Uncle Edwin on the farm. They dealt with major machinery when he was young, and clearly it wasn't as big as the stuff they have nowadays, but it was "big time," and it was deadly. The Lord took care of them through it, so they didn't lose limbs. Phil did a lot of his work with his uncles, Edwin and Selmer, because he liked to be around them. After Uncle Edwin was injured four years later (see page 20), Phil was around Uncle Selmer a lot as they worked in the field for the whole summer. He would take his dad's tractor and go down there to cultivate the corn in his field.

Phil's training in Bible history came as his mother read Bible stories to them every night. It became a regular habit that stuck with

Phil, and we carried it on with our children. As the Lord says, *"And that from a child thou hast known the holy scriptures, which are able to make thee wise unto salvation through faith which is in Christ Jesus"* (2 Timothy 3:15). Phil's mom also taught him how to clean, cook, and wash dishes. After his sisters were gone off to high school, he would sometimes even make meals. Phil later learned from his dad that his mom was overwhelmed after he was born so cooking was a way he could help her.

Phil's mother was also great with discipline, which Phil was sure she learned during her early years as well. She had a willow stick behind the wood stove that she used when necessary—and she used it! If it broke, sometimes the kids would have to go get a new one to be used. She believed in discipline as the Lord said,

> *He that spareth his rod hateth his son:*
> *but he that loveth him chasteneth him betimes.*
> Proverbs 13:24

Phil's mother was concerned about the finances in his growing up years, probably because his dad never made a lot of money. Phil is sure it was because of her growing up days in that large family. The Levorsons always seemed to have enough to get by. While Phil's dad's family lost their farm during the depression, his mom's family probably never knew there was a depression.

Phil remembers observing the Levorson's financial blessings, especially when Uncle Edwin was injured in 1954. Phil was about ten at the time and said he would never forget it because Uncle Selmer was emotionally distraught since he felt responsible for Edwin's injury. Selmer designed and built the lumber saw on the farm himself. Edwin slipped on the ice and got his arm caught in the belt of the saw which caused major damage to Edwin's arm, neck, and body. Edwin was in a Mayo Hospital in Rochester, Minnesota, for several months. At that time there wasn't insurance like we have today, and his hospitalization cost major dollars. Phil was with Selmer when he pulled out of his savings enough to pay for the entire hospital stay. Phil's mother had come from this family that was able to take care of their own, but she did not have that advantage when raising her own children. When Phil was about twelve years old, he remembers spending time just holding his mother's hand as she lay in bed anxious and nervous about household situations and money. It was an emotional time for all of them.

Phil's mom was the apple of her father's eye and seemed to be his favorite as Phil saw it. She and her older brother, Oscar, were the only ones out of fourteen children who went to college at Dr. Martin Luther College (DMLC) in New Ulm. Uncle Oscar was a college-educated professor at DMLC. Phil's mom became a teacher and taught in Lime Creek, Iowa, until she got married in 1935 at twenty-seven years old. She taught again later in life at Messiah Lutheran School in Eau Claire, after she and Phil's dad moved there in 1965.

Phil's Father

As told to me by Phil from his memories of him

Gilbert Raymond Radichel, Phil's dad, was born Thursday, May 5, 1910, in Hortonville, Wisconsin. His parents were Albert Radichel and Matilda (nee Zabel). He was baptized on Sunday, May 29, 1910, and confirmed on Sunday, May 25, 1924. Gilbert was the third of five children by his father's first wife, Matilda: Alvin, Edgar, Gilbert, Anita, and Leona. Gilbert's mother died in 1924 when Gilbert was fourteen years old. His father then married Josephine Zuberbier and they had two children: Carol and Serena. Gilbert's dad, Albert, died when Phil was twenty-one years old. Phil was a pallbearer at his funeral and remembers the event well.

Phil's Dad (1935)

Phil's dad taught him how to work—and work hard! He was a farmer on a farm in Emmons, Minnesota, on the state line between Minnesota and Iowa. After a couple of years on that farm, Phil's parents moved to Lake Mills to live in the house that belonged to Uncle Nels, Valborg's uncle. After Nels died, her brother, Oscar, lived there. Phil's dad farmed there and was a carpenter as well. He worked with Valborg's brother, Ingvald. Phil knows very little about those early days and his father's background, except that his dad worked hard and was a very outgoing man. He would be able to walk up to anyone and start a conversation. Phil felt like his dad knew everyone in Lake Mills, and they knew him.

Gilbert was also very intuitive, according to Phil. He could look at a machine that wasn't working and know immediately what was wrong with it. He would say, "Well, this doesn't look right," and then know what needed to be done. Phil never understood his dad's gifts when he was small, watching him, and didn't think it was anything unusual, but now when he thinks back on it, some of the things that his dad did were, "oh, yeah . . . nobody explained that to him, he just did it." And that's the difference, Phil says. "There are some people that you don't have to explain things to, and other people you have to explain it." His dad also brought them up *in the nurture and admonition of the Lord"* (Ephesians 6:4). Phil says his parents had their priorities squared away.

Phil's parents met at a friend's wedding. Valborg had a friend, Hildegarde Bussmann, while she was at DMLC, and they became close friends. Hildegarde was from Hortonville. When Hildegarde was going to get married to a guy from Hortonville, she asked Valborg to be a member of the bridal party. As it turned out, Hildegarde was getting married to Gilbert's brother, Alvin. I even heard once from Mom Radichel that at one point she and Dad Radichel had to sit in the rumble seat of a car together. Those were the days of the fun cars. But that's how they met. I don't know much more about where it went from there, but I assume it was a long-distance relationship between them. Phil did say they wrote letters, but he never saw a letter that either one wrote to the other. He said his mom would not have kept them.

Phil's parents were married in the living room of the house at Mariland Farm on Sunday, June 9, 1935. Grandpa Levorson was in the throes of colon cancer and in the later stages, so they had the wedding in his home. Gilbert and Valborg lived on a nearby farm in Joyce, Iowa. Margaret, their first child, was born while they lived there. From there they moved to Emmons. Phil said his dad was still a farmer, although he didn't own any land, but rented farmland in Emmons. While in Emmons, three daughters were born: Rebecca, Verona, and Lydia. In 1943, Phil was the next to be born in the hospital at Albert Lea. Around 1944, they moved into Uncle Nels's house which was near Mariland Farm. The first year they were there, Valborg homeschooled the children. The following year Somber

Phil's Parents on their Wedding Day (1935)

Lutheran School was opened, and the school-aged children attended there. Around 1948, they moved to Hortonville, for a short time and then back to Uncle Oscar's house where they had lived before.

In 1960, Gilbert and Valborg moved to a home in Claybank, Minnesota near Red Wing. They had been going through church doctrinal issues in the Norwegian Synod and were going to join the newly-formed Church of the Lutheran Confession (CLC). They had thought about moving to Mankato, Minnesota, where Phil's sister, Verona, was living at the time but couldn't find a place suitable for their needs. His oldest sister, Margaret, and her husband Ray Seeley were living in Red Wing and attending Our Redeemer's Lutheran Church which was part of the CLC. Claybank was a small farm community with a former grocery store that was situated by the railroad tracks. The trains had been discontinued and the store had been made into a residence. The family moved into this residence in June of that year and began attending church at Our Redeemer's.

When the CLC began in 1960, the leaders intended to have a school for the training of students in high school, college, and seminary. During the fall of 1962, Pastor Arvid Gullerud, the pastor at Messiah Lutheran Church in Eau Claire, was made aware of the Ingram Estate in Eau Claire, with several buildings on the seventy-five-acre property. It was going to be sold by a Minnesota foundation that owned it. The amount of the sale was the cost of their remodeling, about $85,000, which meant that this was an unbelievable God-given gift to provide for the new school. The new school campus was dedicated in the fall of 1963 and continued with the name of Immanuel Lutheran College (ILC) with the move from its humble and faithful beginning in Mankato, MN at the start of the synod.

Two years later, Gilbert began working as a maintenance man for ILC in Eau Claire. He rented a trailer as a mobile home and parked it at the Shady Grove Trailer Park for about one year. That year, Phil's two brothers, Fred and Frank, also lived in the trailer as they attended ILC. Valborg began teaching at Messiah Lutheran School in Eau Claire in the fall of 1965 and taught until 1974, missing only one year of teaching during that time.

In 1966, Gilbert purchased a lot on Grover Road across the street from ILC and moved his trailer to that lot. By 1968, he had built a house on the lot with the help of his family. By 1972, Fred and his wife, Naomi, bought a lot on Kim Avenue in Fall Creek, a few miles east of Eau Claire. Phil's parents liked the area and bought the lot across the street from them. Many family members helped with building this house. I remember our son, Brian, had been born in January of that year and we put him in a swing while we helped with the foundation building that spring.

In 1977, while still living on Kim Avenue, Gilbert had a stroke. Fortunately, Fred, who lived directly across the street, came to their house, picked Gilbert up physically, carried him down the steps and drove him to the hospital. Valborg had quit teaching by that time and thus could take care of Gilbert.

In 1985, Gilbert and Valborg moved to a new senior's building called Chardon Court in New Hope, Minnesota, and were now close to both Phil and me as well as Phil's sister, Verona, and her husband, Ed. Verona was the main person who took care of any special needs they had.

In 1986, after my dad, Chuck Sandeen, passed away, Phil and I moved my mother, Ann, to Chardon Court as well. Now all three of them were in the same building. I did enjoy that and even went there occasionally to sing for the residents in their community room. I would get them to sing along with music Daddy taught me. It was music from their generation and many residents enjoyed singing. I asked my voice teacher, Luana Mitchell, to accompany me on the piano, which she graciously did.

After a while, Gilbert and Valborg moved again to an apartment in another senior's building, Caliber Chase, in Crystal, Minnesota, just a couple of miles down the road from Chardon Court. They didn't live there too long before they decided to move back to Chardon Court. Unfortunately, nothing was available there, so they rented an apartment next to Chardon Court. After living in this rental unit a short time, they tried again to move back to Chardon Court. However, the staff at Chardon Court didn't think Valborg was mentally capable of living there anymore.

Within a year, Gilbert and Valborg moved again, this time just across the street from Chardon Court to Pheasant Park Apartments. One winter night at about 10:00 p.m., my mother walked across the street to their building without a coat on and did not understand how to get into their building. She was in the early stages of dementia which we were not aware of at the time. When she couldn't get in the door of their building, because it was a secure building, she went back to her building across the street. She got into the entry of her apartment complex but hadn't brought her key along so she could not get into the lobby area and access the elevators to her apartment. It was a cold, blustery winter night in Minnesota! Fortunately, a man inside the building walked past the front door, saw her trying to get in, recognized her, and let her in. No one told me about this for quite a while. In fact, only when I was moving my mother to a care center down the block from Chardon Court did anyone mention the incident.

Sometime around 1991–92, Verona went to see her parents and found them laughing and enjoying a TV show in the living room. However, she also found a pan of water boiling unattended in the kitchen. It wasn't long after this that Valborg decided it was time for Gilbert to move into a nursing home since it was very difficult for her, or Verona and us, to take care of him. They wanted to go back to Eau Claire, and Valborg wanted to move in with Margaret, their daughter, and her husband, Ray. Gilbert moved into Dove Healthcare in Eau Claire while Valborg moved into the trailer house where Ray and Margaret were living at the time.

It was difficult for Margaret to have her mom living with them, even though Valborg wanted to be there. Valborg would get up in the middle of the night, put her coat on, and try to leave. Margaret would have trouble sleeping lots of nights wondering what her mother was doing. At one point Ray and Margaret were going to go on a vacation so Valborg went to stay at Dove Healthcare with Gilbert. After that, Valborg decided she wanted to move into Dove with Gilbert. She said they had been together for almost sixty years, so why wouldn't she keep doing that? Problem solved!

On Saturday, June 24, 1995, we had a sixtieth wedding anniversary celebration for Gilbert and Valborg. There were fifty-five family members there to celebrate their anniversary.

Phil's Parents 60th Wedding Anniversary (1995)

On Sunday, July 30, 1995, just five weeks later, Gilbert passed away as a result of an aneurysm. The victory service for Gilbert Raymond Radichel was held at Messiah Lutheran Church in Eau Claire, on Tuesday, August 1, 1995, followed by his interment in Prairie View Cemetery in the township of Hallie, Wisconsin. What a joy it was to have had the Lord give us all that special anniversary time with both of them before He called Gilbert home. Thank You, Lord!

Valborg continued to live at Dove Healthcare until she passed away on Friday, April 12, 2002, only a couple of weeks after Phil's sister, Lydia, had passed away on Thursday, March 21st. During these last couple of years at Dove, Valborg had fallen out of bed, broken her hip, and had surgery to repair it. She often talked about working in the kitchen at Dove—saying she did that, but that was not the case. We know that she would have done that joyfully, if she had been able both physically and mentally.

The victory service for Valborg Amanda (Levorson) Radichel was held at Messiah Lutheran Church in Eau Claire, on Monday, April 15, 2002. That same day she was laid to rest next to her husband in Prairie View Cemetery. Thank You, Lord, for the Christian example of this woman.

Train up a child in the way he should go:
and when he is old, he will not depart from it.
Proverbs 22:6

Born to parents God had chosen,
Their examples trained us well.
By God's Word their lives were fashioned,
In His grace we learned to dwell.

As we grew in His protection,
As we watched our parents live,
And their labors for His kingdom
From their heart and soul would give.

Chapter 2

Our Childhood

From a child thou hast known the holy scriptures,
which are able to make thee wise unto salvation
through faith which is in Christ Jesus.

2 Timothy 3:15

P hil and I both grew up similarly—poor materially, but rich spiritually. For that we continually thank our Lord. Each of us came from a country setting and had parents who didn't have much money. Everyone worked hard to make a living, but we were always blessed with food on the table.

Phil's Childhood

Phil's parents, Gilbert and Valborg, were blessed with seven children: Margaret, Rebecca, Verona, Lydia, Philip, Frederick, and Frank. Four girls were followed by three boys, with Phil being the oldest boy. Phil was born in Albert Lea, Minnesota about 15 miles from where his parents lived in Emmons, Minnesota. His father was a farm worker in the area as well as a carpenter. Although his mother had been a teacher before, she did not teach while she was raising her family. Phil says he doesn't remember anything during this time in Emmons as he was very young. Not too long ago he said to me, "It would be fun to get to a little town and go into a hardware store. I do remember a hardware store my dad would go to in Emmons—the old wood floors that would creak when you walked on them." We were driving through northern Iowa at the time and suddenly this past reflection just hit him from years gone by. Those are the memories I like to try to keep.

A short time after Phil was born, his family moved from Emmons to Lake Mills, Iowa near the homestead where his mother grew up. Uncle Oscar's house was within a half mile walking distance to the homestead, called Mariland Farm. Halfway between the house and the farm was Somber Lutheran Church and School where the family worshiped and Phil went to grade school. The family cemetery was behind the church.

Phil often talks about his life growing up in the country, the dangers of farming, and how much he learned just being near the machinery. Around the age of four or five he was driving Uncle Edwin's tractor and ended up running into a fence post. He did love the machinery and the fact that his uncles let him use it. He helped a lot on the farm early on and remembers raking leaves in the church cemetery and putting them in Uncle Selmer's manure spreader. His job was to get in and step them down. Uncle Selmer would spread the leaves on the fields. Phil thought that was a very effective way to get rid of them.

Some of the early memories Phil has about the Iowa farm involve an old barn that was collapsing. His dad, a carpenter, knew how to take care of this so they tore it down and built a new one. The new barn was smaller but it would hold a couple of cows. It had a little hayloft out of which Phil's brother, Frank, fell one time. Yes, Frank did recover from the fall. It was also the place where his dad once was troweling concrete. Phil was holding the light with two hands and touched a bare wire. A shock went through his whole body. His dad yelled at him, "Drop it! Drop it!" Phil couldn't until finally his body collapsed which made him then drop the light. The shock was so severe that he could hardly walk to the house, but he did survive it.

In the early 1950s, life was different on a farm. Phil talks about those days when his dad and uncles farmed the way their fathers did, and their farms were more self-sufficient. They didn't need much from the outside world. What they needed was electricity which was brought in by the wire. They needed flour, because they didn't grind their own, and gas for the tractors. But they had a large barrel for gas which, when filled, would last a month or more. They grew most of their food and had cows for milk. They even made their own butter. In today's world the farms are so big and so mechanized that the farmers can't even fix their equipment but must call for help. Now, he says, when we go to Iowa to Mariland Farm and ask, "Who's farming the land now?" it's usually some guy who lives in the area who is farming everything around, thousands of acres, which are leased out to him or are in sharecropping. Phil has often talked about wanting to farm, even when he was young, but always knew you had to have money and his parents never had enough. As much as I, too, loved the country and spent some of my growing up years living in homes that were in a country setting, I'm thankful that we didn't have the responsibility of a farm when we were raising our children. We were able to take them places and see things that helped them appreciate all of God's creation.

Of course, Phil's uncles didn't have time to go anywhere as they were always doing farm work year-round. Uncle Selmer didn't take a big trip until he was the last one on the farm. He took a bus trip to Door County, Wisconsin, because he always wanted to go there. Phil often comments on how brilliant Uncle Selmer was and with only an eighth grade education, although he is not even sure Uncle Selmer went that far. When he talks about his own dad, he says, "I'm not sure if he finished high school, but there was a street-smart, very smart individual!" My own thought is, "And acorns don't fall far from the tree!"

Phil does remember that he and his family made a couple of trips when he was young. He remembers driving to the Black Hills. He also remembers going to Hortonville, Wisconsin, to visit his dad's family, when he had to stand up in the back seat since there wasn't enough room for him to sit down. One trip he made was with his Uncle Oscar and Uncle Earnest Renbeck, who had arthritis. Uncle Oscar was taking Uncle Earnest to Montana to sit in a mine. It seems the minerals from the mine would be able to help his arthritis.

Although Phil says he doesn't remember much before he was five years old, he does remember when his mother's nephew, Arnold Holt, and his wife, Elaine, came to the farm when Uncle Nels was dying. Phil thinks Elaine was a nurse and helped his mom take care of Uncle Nels. This happened before their family moved to Hortonville.

Speaking of Hortonville, there was a short time, less than a year, when Phil's family moved to Hortonville before Phil started school. During this time, Phil's older sister, Verona, told me that Phil and his younger brother, Fred, thought they found a gopher hole and stuck a hose down it only to end up flooding the basement of a cottage on the property. They were probably just trying to help get rid of the gophers.

Phil started first grade at age six, while they were in Hortonville, but doesn't remember much about grade school. He does remember starting school there and went two to three weeks before they moved back to Mariland Farm in Lake Mills.

Back on the farm again, he was now in school at Somber Lutheran School. As a first grader there were fifteen to sixteen kids in the whole school, most of them Phil's relatives. At one recess they were playing the game of "Kick the Can" and Phil got to be "it." The object of the game was for the students to run and hide and wait for a time to run in and touch the can and yell their name and be free. As each student ran in from hiding to touch the can, the person who was "it" had to beat them to the can and say their name first to win.

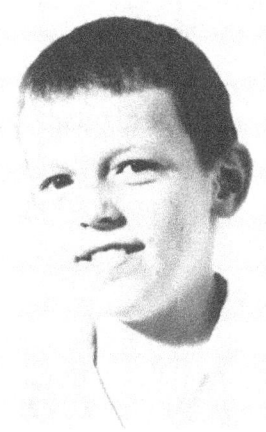

On this particular day, all the students came running in at once and since Phil couldn't reach the can and yell all their names before they got in, he lost and had to be "it" again. He got frustrated with this repetition and had to go pick up the can, put it down, and start over again each time. Eventually, the teacher decid-

Phil in the early grade school days (~1950)

ed that this was enough and wasn't going to let them do this again. So, he stopped them from running to hide when suddenly Phil, with can in hand, turned around and threw it at the kids. It was a big can and Phil was only a first grader, but his cousin, Erwin Levorson, didn't duck and the can hit him in the forehead and gashed him. He ended up needing four to five stitches. Phil said, "My mother wanted me to apologize to him, but I didn't want to. I don't think she ever found out I didn't apologize."

Phil has commented that he felt bad for his younger brothers later in his life since they had no opportunity to work on the farm as he had. His dad would say to him, "This field needs tilling!" and Phil got off school to do it. He had a spring-tooth drag to do the field. He went back and forth across the field more than once. The ground was well-prepared and finally done. That cornfield was the one he and his father planted by moonlight. Phil stood on the tractor between his dad's feet as his dad would shift. While on the tractor together, Phil recalled that there was "nary a word" spoken between them. But that was the interesting thing about his father—he did not talk to Phil very much at all, except to give him direction. The field had been so finely spring-toothed that by the fourth of July the corn tasseled out about eight feet. The people walking out of church would stop and ask his dad, "What did you do there?" Phil didn't think his dad understood that it wasn't the planting by moonlight, but rather all the extra spring-toothing (which got him out of school) that made all the difference. It was funny, though, he said his dad was so proud of that cornfield, you would not believe it. Likewise, Phil was so surprised that that cornfield was so high in comparison to all the other cornfields around it—which were not nearly as high. When I asked him what his mom thought, he said she never heard anything at all—ever—about this event. He thought he was about ten at the time and clearly he knew never to speak about it—having been so late at night. The thing that was interesting, he thought, was that they didn't need lights on the tractor because the moon was so bright.

Phil's sister, Verona, told us a funny story about that same field when she went to their cousin Red's funeral. She had talked to Komer Groh—a neighbor—about the field. Komer said he bought that plot after Red sold it and that there was never another plot of land around there that grew corn like that one did! He said it was just amazing. It still gets the best corn in the whole area. He didn't know what it was, but the soil had to be just perfect for that corn!

When Phil was older, before his dad's stroke, their relationship was more "I need some help" when his dad needed to borrow money from him. Then after Dad's stroke, when the folks lived on Kim Avenue near Eau Claire, Wisconsin, late one evening we went to see Dad. Dad and Phil were alone in another room. Dad started talking to Phil about his remorse or his concern about how he had treated all his children, and he needed to get it off his chest. Phil tried to help him through his confession by telling him it was OK. Reflecting on this moment of Phil with his father makes me more adamant about reaching out to our children as we continue to watch the hand of the Lord in our own maturing lives.

Phil has commented to me about this particular time that unlike his dad, his mother, who didn't show emotion, showed the stress by saying, "I can't handle it anymore" rather than by using sobs of emotion. Phil said, "Very interesting woman, that woman was—a strict disciplinarian—and didn't hesitate to use the willow stick when we were younger. I can tell you now that when I was in eighth grade and all my sisters were gone, and I was holding her hand as she was lying in bed somewhat sobbing and very distraught, my sensation was she was very ill and I was quite concerned about her." But Phil also said, "As she was much, much older, and as a son having to deal with her in her failing years, she was much more insecure."

One thing I especially remember Phil telling me about his parents concerning money is that every fall, when it was time to send their kids off to Doctor Martin Luther College (DMLC) in New Ulm, Minnesota, his dad would go to the bank to borrow the money to pay for their high school education. I had wanted to go to DMLC when I was ready for high school. My brother was there too. But my parents said they "couldn't afford it." That came back to me many times after Phil and I were dating and Phil told me what his parents had done for them. But as I look back on all my thoughts on this subject and the numerous times over the years that I have mentioned this to others in a complaining way, I can only say thank you to my Lord for the lesson I learned the hard way to forgive and forget. He has used this lesson for me to remind me that . . .

All things work together for good to them that love God, to them who are the called according to his purpose.
Romans 8:28

Phil was able to go to DMLC as a high school freshman. He played football there and made a lot of good friends. In the middle of his junior year of high school, after his family had left the Norwegian

Synod, Phil transferred to Immanuel Lutheran High School (ILHS) in Mankato, Minnesota, and his parents moved to Red Wing. It was during this time that I first met Phil.

Jackie's Childhood

My parents were blessed with my brother, Jim, and me. They were also blessed to be able to help raise Mom's sister, Shirley, after my grandmother, Mom and Shirley's mother, died after Shirley's birth. For several years, Shirley lived in Sioux City, Iowa, with her father, my Grandpa Otto, and her sister, Mildred, who had gotten married to Lynn Briley. They were also my godparents. Shirley would often go back and forth between Grandpa Otto/Aunt Mid's house and our house, mostly coming to our house in the summer. Shirley finally came to live with us in her high school years. She always was like a sister to me.

It is often said the first five years of one's life is seldom remembered, that we are too young to retain much. On the contrary, there are many things I have never forgotten about my early years. Although I do not remember living in Sioux City until I was eighteen months old, I do remember getting my picture taken there when I was about a year old.

Two things stick in my mind vividly. The first thing I remember was this flower someone put in my mouth. I was supposed to hold it in my teeth and smile so they could snap the picture. I will tell you that smiling while holding a

At 1 Year, I loved to smile. (1946)

flower between my teeth was difficult enough, but even more difficult was doing it while tasting the flower, which tasted awful—bitter, prickly, and wet. Despite all that, the picture turned out great!

The other vivid remembrance I have of that picture session, being a happy, smiley child, was the all-out effort to make me pout! It seems the photographers, two sisters my mother knew, often remarked to Mom that

They worked hard to make 1-year-old me pout. (1946)

they had never seen me crying or even pouting. Their goal was to get me to look sad and unhappy. Mom told me how they tried pinching me and scolding me but still I would only laugh at them. (This type of laughter followed me to my teens and was mimicked by my own daughter later.) At last, they accomplished their goal and snapped the picture. My mother kept this framed trophy on her whatnot, and it remains on the same shelf to this day, now in my living room.

Since I have so many memories of the many places I lived growing up, I am going to give some of my most memorable highlights of each place. The first place I remember was Military Road in Sioux City, where I was born. The only reason I think I remember anything about this place is that I have a picture of it in Mom's old picture album, and she talked about it a lot. When I was a teenager and our family would go back to Sioux City to see the relatives, we would occasionally drive by the house. That's what I remember about it. Dad was working for the government at the time and got a job up in Minnesota working for a candy company.

We moved to Somerset, Wisconsin, which was across the river from St. Paul, Minnesota. We lived at Whispering Pines in a cabin by the Apple River, and Mom would go down to the river to bring up water by the bucket. She would boil the water so she could use it for general purposes in the kitchen. I remember we lived there during the winter months as well, and when she went down to get the water, she had to chop a hole in the ice first to get the bucket in the water. The cabin was a log cabin, and in the winter the snow would blow through the cracks in the logs. The part of the cabin I was sleeping in didn't have any chinking between all the logs and would let the snow come in on top of my crib blankets. In the morning Mom would shake the snow from my blankets and give me my clothes to put on. She had hung them by the oil burner furnace we had in the middle of the cabin to warm them before I could put them on.

We moved to an apartment over a bar in this Somerset community for a little while. The bar was on a street corner with the steps on the corner of the building coming up to the front door of the bar at an angle. There was a metal bar sign that hung just outside our apartment window on the street side. Every time the wind blew a little, that sign would squeak as it rocked back and forth. I could actually fall asleep to that squeaking noise. I remember that at one point a car went out of control on the main street and drove up the corner steps of that building. Since we were in the upstairs apartment, it was no problem for us.

From there we moved to Ellsworth, Wisconsin. Dad was still working for the candy company, I believe. The house we lived in there was big compared to all we had lived in before. It was out in the country, and we had an outhouse we had to use in the daytime. At night, Mom had a pot Jim and I could use in our bedroom if we needed to go to the bathroom. There was one furnace in the middle of the lower level that heated the whole house. Our bedrooms were heated only by the air that came up the steps from the lower level.

We had a large lot with neighbors behind us way up the hill on a farm. They were the Froisland family. We called the older man Uncle

Oliver. He was the first one to teach me about dipping bread in Karo syrup and eating it. What a great snack that was! We would walk up to their house through the fields if they hadn't been planted yet. Shirley was with us at times during the summer, and I remember her mowing the lawn. At one point a snake popped its head above the ground, and as she mowed over it, she cut its head off. She was so scared she ran back down to the house. I also remember a birthday party Mom had for me there. I think it was my third birthday.

After Ellsworth, we moved to Hay Creek, Minnesota. This was just outside of Red Wing, Minnesota. We lived high up on a hill in a farmhouse, but we didn't have anything to do with the farm. There was also a machine shed on the property that held equipment for the farm. The entry to our place was a long driveway lined on both sides with apple trees. The house was a two-story classic farmhouse with indoor water that you got through a hand pump in the kitchen. We did have a bathroom upstairs by our bedrooms. Shirley and Jim went to school at Immanuel Lutheran Church in Hay Creek, a Lutheran Church Missouri Synod (LCMS) German Lutheran grade school. I was not in school yet at that time.

Some of the things I remember most about this place were the wind-storms because we were so high on the hill. One storm took several of the apple trees in the driveway and laid the walls of the machine shed on their sides with the roof coming to rest on top of the machinery. We also had no refrigeration, so Mom had to keep the milk in the cistern out by the windmill. This was a deep waterproof tank that would help keep food or water cooler than the outside temperature. At one point we were pulling up a bottle of milk and the rope slipped. The bottle dropped and broke, spilling the milk all over the floor of the cistern. We had to get a ladder, go down into the deep tank, and clean it out.

Mom's Uncle Harry surprised us and came one Thanksgiving with turkey for the meal and gifts for everyone. He gave Mom a full set of kitchen carving knives which she had until she retired and had to get rid of them. Uncle Harry was so much fun. We played Blind Man's Bluff and even my dad got into it. Uncle Harry even got up on the dining room table to avoid getting tagged by my dad. What fun we had! At Christmas, Dad's sister Doris—we called her Aunt Janey—came with her husband Elmer and brought gifts for all of us. I got a robe and slippers which I wore for years! Our closest neighbors were the Augustine's who lived across the road and owned most of the farmland around us.

It was also at this place that my mother made a pumpkin pie and set it on the steps overnight to cool. My Grandpa Otto was staying with us at the time. When Mom went to get the pie on the steps, it was gone. She found out that Grandpa Otto was hungry and had eaten the whole pie. Needless to say, she wasn't happy about it but still chuckled over the story whenever she told it.

From my mother, I had learned the joy of singing and gave it all the gusto my heart held. It seemed to make other people happy, and sometimes I'd even hear some people clap. At one point, while we were living in Hay Creek, Mom took me to an event and let me go on a stage to sing to a whole bunch of people. Now that was fun!!! I remember singing Zip-A-Dee-Doo-Dah and several other songs I knew. People kept clapping, so I kept singing. Soon I ran out of songs I knew, so I yelled out to Mom, "What else, Mom?" This brought a lot of laughter and my mother running on stage and swooping me off. That was the end of my singing debut. But as I look back, I can see the hand of the Lord encouraging me continually in my singing. Thank You, Lord, for the joy of sharing this blessing from You.

We seemed to live only a year or so at each place. I think we mostly rented each place. We then moved into Red Wing and lived at 614 College Avenue in the lower half of a two-story duplex. This was only a few blocks from St. John's Lutheran Church where Jim went to school. I wasn't in school yet. While we lived here, Shirley came to stay for the summer. She took care of Jim and me since Mom was working during the day. We would occasionally go for walks up and down the city blocks. One time I specifically remember: while we were on our walk, Shirley suddenly remembered she had left the water running to fill the tub for a bath. We ran back to the house and shut off the water. It had reached the top of the tub and would have run over in a few more minutes. Shirley was so glad she remembered it. The tub was an old-fashioned deep tub and held a lot of water!

Other things I clearly remember while living there included Jim and I having whooping cough. I think I whooped for months after we got well. On Christmas while we were there, a knock came at the door. When Mom opened the door, a man gave her a gift for me. It was a doll. I didn't play with dolls much, but what a kind person to do that. Mom said later that one of the city organizations would go around the city giving gifts to kids.

There was a brand-new house next to us up the street where a senior lady lived. We would talk to her occasionally when we were outside. My Mom knew her. I was at her home one day, and she saw me biting my fingernails. She came over to me, grabbed my hand and said, "What boy would ever want to put a ring on those fingers?" Whoa. I stopped biting my nails that very day! It amazes me as I watch the hand of the Lord taking care of me each and every day, even for the little things of life. Years later, when I was getting married and a ring was being put on my finger, I thought of this sweet lady. Thank You, Lord, for sending her into my life.

Our next house was 1224 Phelps Street in Red Wing, up toward the city cemetery. It was now 1950. I was going into kindergarten and would attend Hancock Elementary School. So many new friends to meet and many of those friendships lasted through high school and throughout my life. Shirley was living with us all the time now but would go back to Sioux City at times to stay with her other sisters and brothers for a week or so in the summer. One thing I especially remember happened to Shirley while we lived on Phelps Street. She had been to a movie called King Solomon's Mine and that night in bed she woke up screaming. She was so loud she woke everyone up. Mom had all she could do to calm her down. I don't think she ever went to another horror movie again.

Lots of memories occurred while living in this house, even though we only lived there a year. Shirley was confirmed at St. John's Lutheran Church. Grandpa Otto would come up to go fishing, and he and I would go by the Edgewater Bar on the Island to fish in the river there. The Watsons lived across the street from us. They owned the little grocery store at the end of the block. Their daughter, Marilyn, was in my class in kindergarten and later in high school.

Behind the Watson's house lived the Knutsen family. Bobby and Jimmy Knutsen were the sons of Bob and Marcella. They also went to St. John's Church, at least Marcella and the boys did. My brother Jim was in the same class as Bobby. All the boys went to St. John's Grade School together and were great buddies. Marcella and Mom were friends. Neither their dad nor our dad was a member at St. John's. One of the things that happened, by the grace of God and through this family friendship over the years is that our dads began going to adult confirmation class at St. John's with Pastor George Barthels.

A year later, 1951, we moved to 206 East 5th Street. I was going into first grade, thinking it would be at St. John's Grade School. However, Colville Grade School was only a few blocks down the street, and Mom thought it would be good for Jim to go to a public school for one year and he and I could walk to school. Jim wasn't too pleased with that idea but didn't have much he could do or say about it. Mom said later in life that it was good for him to have that experience since he wanted to be a pastor and could see what goes on in a public school. A wise woman she was.

Our next-door neighbors, Johnny and Hulda Johnson, were very dear Scandinavian people. We got along great with them, and I would go over to visit with them often. Hulda had a hutch filled with decorative teacups and saucers. She would let me have milk in them when she had her tea. She knew how much I loved the color purple and gave me one of her Scandinavian sets to keep. I still have it in my hutch to this day. When Phil and I got married, their daughter brought a gift to my parents' door before the wedding. She said it was something that Hulda wanted only me to have—not even her daughter was allowed to take it or use it. It was a white linen tablecloth that Hulda had from her home. I also have that tablecloth to this day.

Our house on 5th Street was below the big hill called Barn Bluff or Mt. LaGrange. It was a real mountain as it was 1,001 feet above sea level. What adventures Jim and I had with the Knutsen boys roaming on Barn Bluff. They still came to visit us a lot during the summer, and Jim and I would take them up to the caves in the hill and do a lot of exploring. Looking back on it, it was very dangerous doing that with all the snakes and animals that lived in them. Thankfully the Lord was always looking out for us.

One time when we were playing on top of the hill, we tied ourselves together with rope as real explorers did. We were at a point where we couldn't see anything in front of us—we hadn't been that far down that end of the mountain before. We rolled a few rocks down the hill but didn't know where they had gone. Fortunately, I accidentally stepped in a gopher hole and turned my ankle. Jim came back, untied me from the ropes, and decided we would all go back down the way we came up the hill so he could take me home. He always did take care of me! Much later, as we were in the car going to Colville Park, we could see where we had been on top of the hill. If we had continued for less than a block, the first kid may have fallen off the edge of the hill, since you couldn't see an edge to it. It dropped straight down several hundred feet to the rocks below. If the first kid would have gone over the edge, the ropes would have pulled each of the rest of us over as well. The Lord certainly was not ready for us at that time! We had work left to do in His kingdom. Thank You, Lord!

For he shall give his angels charge over thee,
to keep thee in all thy ways.
They shall bear thee up in their hands,
lest thou dash thy foot against a stone.
Psalm 91:11–12

Finally, in 1953, the last place we moved to while Jim and I were still living at home was *Sandy Acres* on Twin Bluff Road. The hill behind the house had been cut back just enough to build the house's foundation. Also on the property away from the house was the start of another foundation that the original owner was going to build something on, but it was never built. To Dad and Mom, who loved to work and could do lots of carpentry things, this was a great buy. All summer long we worked on finishing the kitchen floor, installing the cupboards, putting in a septic tank, and drilling a well. A concrete step was poured so we could get in the front door. At last, we got to move in.

After we lived there a while, Dad and Mom allowed Mom's friend, Vera Everhart, and her mom, Bell, to move their trailer house on to our property. They placed it under the trees on the side lawn so the trailer would be cooler in the summer and warmer in the winter. Vera met my mother several years before when they both worked at the Knitting Mills. Vera and Bell had moved to Red Wing from Correctionville, Iowa, where my dad was from, after Bell was divorced. Bell's sister, Edna, and her husband, Milt Warren, along with her sister, Carol, lived in Red Wing at the time. Vera and Mom had become good friends. They also bowled on the same team. At the time I first remember them, they lived behind the gas station on Main Street next to what is now the Dairy Queen.

I remember Bell taking me to Edna Warren's house several times. At one point they were all having coffee and asked me if I wanted any. I must have been around five or six at the time. It was in the summertime, so I wasn't in school. I accepted a cup that they had made for me, and they had added a lot of cream with sugar. One taste of that coffee and I have NEVER had another cup of coffee, not even a sip! I did NOT like it at all!

I always loved being around Vera and Bell. Besides getting to go to their relatives' home, I would get to do things with Vera. When Uncle Earl, Mom's brother, bought Jim a horse, we had to fence in the upper part of the acreage so Jim's horse would have room to run for exercise and eat the grass. He needed a barn to sleep in and get out of any inclement weather. Uncle Earl's brother-in-law, Bert Curtis, came to do the major work on the barn. It was the summer of 1954. I don't remember how long it was before Vera and Bert were married, but when that happened, Bell moved to California where she had other relatives and where she later died. Vera and Bert moved to Everett, Washington for quite a while until Bert passed away. After that, Vera moved out East to Pennsylvania to live with a friend of hers, Monica, and her husband, Matt Springer. Vera passed away in 2018 at the age of ninety-seven. Thank You, Lord, for the joy of knowing these people.

As for Copper, Jim's horse, he was another addition to the animals we had on the homestead. We had started with a dog named Sport. We didn't have Sport too long. He was always running out in the road and barking at the cars. One day as Vera was coming home from work, Sport raced out to her car and scared Vera. She swerved and hit him, and he died. She felt so bad! Then we got a new puppy, Rex—a little black runt of the litter. Jimmy loved him so much. He was a great protector of us and wouldn't let anyone hurt us. Mom couldn't even spank us when Rex was around. I think she was a little afraid of him. Jim would dress Rex up in his winter jacket, and Rex would smile.

We even took this picture of Rex smiling as he had one leg up on the edge of the step, just as if he were having a conversation with you. Rex was a real friend and certainly a companion to us as we roamed the hills and caves around the city. Many years later, we had to put him down because of his age and physical problems. We buried him under the tree where we had our tree house and tree swing. I sang "Old Shep" over his grave using Rex in place of Shep in the song.

My brother, Jim, told Rex a funny joke! (1951)

What freedom Jimmy and I had! Mom worked in those days when most other moms were at home with their children. So, Jim and I got to roam all over, as long as we were home before she got home from work. We built forts, tree houses, and fenced-in areas for the horses up in the hills behind our house. We'd ride in the hills and valleys, often with Freddie Reichert, a neighbor, and his horse, Trigger. What fun those summers were—riding free.

Mom wanted to dig out more behind the house, so we would have some backyard and some flat ground around the house. She decided to make terraces as she dug the dirt out to make more room as the hill got steeper. We shoveled a lot that summer, moving the dirt from the back of the house to the front lawn to build it up level. We all worked at it every spare minute we had. This was also the time that Jim got Copper and the barbed wire fence went up. Funny thing about putting up the wire, it ran right across the path we used to go to the neighbor's house next door, Jim and Donna Lee Fairbanks. When I would go over there to play, I would always come back and have to crawl through the barbed wire fence to get home. One Sunday, as I was running on the path and looking back at my friend who was following me, I felt something touch my cheek and turned quickly as I tried to stop. The barb from the upper fence sliced through my cheek and across my nose. I immediately put my hands up to my cheeks, crawled through the fence and ran down to where Mom was digging dirt. When she saw me coming with blood running down my cheeks through my fingers, she yelled for Dad who was laying foundation blocks for our new garage he was building. He came running to help. When Mom pulled my hands away, my cheek fell down a ways and more blood came. Dad helped me down the terrace while Mom ran in to call a doctor.

It seems on that Sunday afternoon, there weren't many doctors around our small town since most of them had gone to a doctors convention in the Twin Cities. The clinic did find one available, Dr. Wasmund, who said he would meet us at the clinic, so Dad and Mom rushed me there. The doctor took one look at my cheek and started to swab it so he could stitch it up. Mom never could handle a lot of blood, so she went out in the hall to wait. Since it was Sunday and no one else was at the clinic, Dad provided the services of a nurse for Dr. Wasmund. After dropping a few drops of Novocaine into the open wound, he began to stitch me up. It was very close to my eye so he told me I could close my eyes—but I didn't. I wanted to watch what he was doing. Twenty-seven stitches later he was finished, and I was bandaged up, ready to go home. This was in August 1954, when I was nine and a couple of weeks before I would be going back to school, starting the fourth grade. As it turned out, Mom found out later that Doctor Wasmund happened to be the only plastic surgeon in town. He had told my folks that if it didn't look good by the time I was sixteen, I could come back and he would open it up and do it over again. I never went back. Of course, I had to listen to kids in school calling me "scar face" for quite a while, which didn't help my self-confidence in my teen years.

My brother, Jim, and I had many great experiences together growing up. After his confirmation in 1957, when it came time for him to go off to ninth grade in high school, he went to DMLC. He had decided many years earlier that he wanted to be a minister, after hearing Pastor Norbert Reim speak at a Mission Festival. I remember helping to get his clothes and things together that he would need. Mom got him a metal suitcase (footlocker) and filled it with new clothes.

The day came for him to leave, and we all got into the car. New Ulm was about a three-hour drive from Red Wing. Jim seemed excited to go. The city wasn't much different in size compared to Red Wing and the school was on top of a big hill. Also on top of that hill was a statue of Hermann the German, which was very tall. You could go up to the bottom of the platform that he was on and see out over the whole city. Even from miles away as you were driving to New Ulm you could see the statue.

When we reached the boys' dorm where Jim would stay, we were all allowed to take his things upstairs to see his room. I don't remember much more about that until we got ready to leave. It finally sunk in that he was staying, and we were going home without him. I didn't like having to leave him and wasn't sure what I was going to do at home without him. As we left New Ulm, I was turned around in the backseat (no seatbelts needed in those days) with my chin on my arms, watching out the back window until I could no longer see the statue of Herman in the park next to campus. What a long, quiet ride home that was. Jim was starting a new adventure away from home while I was losing my best friend, my hero, and my protector. We have always been close and still are to this day. But I still had a couple of years in grade school yet to complete. This chapter of my life was coming to an end, and I felt abandoned.

Trust in the LORD with all thine heart;
and lean not unto thine own understanding.
Proverbs 3:5

Grade school at St John's Lutheran School was easy and fun for me. I especially enjoyed the singing at church services and our wonderful Christmas concerts. When I got to the seventh grade, I was in the special choir that did extra numbers during the Christmas service. We had a large school so taking ten to fifteen kids out for a special choir wasn't a problem. We sang descants during the actual Luke 2 Christmas story that enhanced the telling of the story. It was a wonderful experience that I will never forget. I felt so very special to be asked to sing in that choir.

My teachers during my years at St John's were Miss Preuter in grades two and three, Mr. Voigt in grade four, Mr. Sieg in grades five and six, and Mr. Voigt again in grade seven. During the summer of 1958, we left St John's for doctrinal reasons and were part of the new church formed by members who left St John's. This church was named Our Redeemer's Lutheran Church. Several members of the new congregation had found and purchased a large lot with a house on it. They were going to have a new church built on this lot. We held services in the basement of the home of a family, Mr. and Mrs. Arnold Raasch, for several months until the congregation had finished building the church.

I didn't have to skip a beat between seventh and eighth grades because they started a grade school within a couple of weeks from leaving St John's. The school was held in the study of the house which stood on the lot purchased by the church. Two of my former teachers who also left St John's, Mr. Walmar Voigt and Mr. Alvin Sieg, shared the teaching duties of our school and taught half time, while working the other part of their day in a different job for their family expenses. What a blessing to watch the hand of the Lord as He took care of all of us. By Christmas of 1958, we were in our new church building. The thirteen students in all eight grades did the entire Christmas Eve service, which included special music for all of us. It was such a joy to participate in this service.

My pastor through my entire grade school years was Pastor George Barthels. He was so inspirational to me during these very important, developmental years of my life. I watched as he instructed my father and baptized and confirmed him. I watched as he confirmed my brother. I watched as he left a synod that was going astray from God's Word and then be called to a new startup congregation, in which my family was also involved. He did all my confirmation instruction and firmly led me in the truth of the Scriptures. Now in our new church he was confirming me in this true biblical doctrine of Holy Scripture. He told our class of three confirmands he was doing something he had never done before. He was going to let us choose our own confirmation verse. He wanted us to use what we had learned to choose a passage that would truly mean something to us for life. After going through a number of passages, I chose a passage that I had learned and that would take me into my adulthood and beyond:

> *Seek ye first the kingdom of God, and his righteousness; and all these things shall be added unto you.*
> Matthew 6:33

I felt that this verse summed up everything I had been taught by my parents as well as by my teachers and pastor over the years. If I could just remember to weigh everything I would do in light of what God asked me to do, I would be taken care of by Him for whatever He deemed I would need in my life. I have tried to live by this principle each day in my life. And as I watch the hand of the Lord, all I can say is, "To God be the glory!"

In this light, getting ready for my confirmation was a unique experience for both me and my mother. Our class of three included another girl, Sally Ferber, and a boy, Emery Fitschen. Mom wanted Sally and me to have matching dresses so that after the service, for the reception and pictures, we would look alike. She bought material and made the dresses. They were all white with white satin ribbon on the full skirt.

Mom had always cut and fixed my hair. Sally had very long, dark-brown, straight and somewhat oily hair. My mother asked Sally's mom if she could fix Sally's hair for the service. Sally's mom said yes. So, Saturday before the Sunday morning service, my mother cut Sally's hair, gave her a permanent, and fixed her hair. I had put pin curls in my hair Friday night, and Mom said it would be fine for Sunday.

When we got to church Sunday morning, Sally had a crinoline under her skirt, and her hair was beautiful! My hair was okay, and my skirt was straight with no fluff. Sally got lots of compliments. It didn't help my self-confidence much, but I often think back to it as a lesson the Lord taught me through my mother about taking care of others first! Thank You, Lord!

During my eighth grade year, I started work like most girls do with babysitting. My most steady babysitting came while working for a high school teacher who had a daughter who was not in school. I don't remember how old she was, but they lived on our road. As I would walk home from school, yes, "uphill both directions," I would pass their house and see her playing outside. One day one of the parents saw me and asked me if I did any babysitting. I said, "yes," and the jobs started coming in. I believe I got fifteen to twenty cents an hour, but one New Year's Eve, a year or two later, when the parents came home around 1:00 a.m., they gave me over twenty dollars for the five to six hours I was there. WOW! That was the most money I had ever made!

My brother and I were part of what our group of Red Wing friends called the TBCC or Twin Bluff Country Club. We usually met in the basement recreation room in the home of Fred Reichert. Fred was my age and lived on Twin Bluff Road as well. Fred's family had a horse or two on their property like we did. There were several other friends, both mine and my brother's, who lived on this road too. We would get together most weekends and more often during the summers. The Reicherts also owned a cabin on the Island close to Red Wing. During summer months, the group would go there to party, water ski, and just hang out. Reicherts would also allow us to use this shoreline for some of our church get-togethers. Because of the friendships we had in the TBCC, I was asked by one of the freshman high school guys to the Feather Frolic, a high school dance, as an eighth grader. The guy I went with was a great dancer and I loved to dance, just like my Daddy did! I had a good time and got to meet a lot of my future classmates.

When I got into high school, I turned to waitressing at Hutch's café on the corner of the street by the entrance to what would be the new Eisenhower Bridge. I believe I made around seventy-five cents an hour, but the tips would be the real money during my shift—maybe ten to twenty-five cents for each person I waited on. After three years of slinging hash (which was excellent food by the way), I had enough money to purchase my first good winter coat. It was PURPLE (Red Wing High School color) and had a real SILVER (my second favorite color) Fox collar. The coat cost me eighty dollars! I wore that coat for thirty or more years until the Silver Fox collar started shedding so I took it off and wore it without a collar, just a colorful scarf instead. There were no buttons on the coat since it was a clutch coat. I liked that since I seldom buttoned a coat anyway, and I still don't! I could not ever throw that coat away and eventually donated it. I knew someone else would get additional use out of it.

> But godliness with contentment is great gain. For we brought nothing into this world, and it is certain we can carry nothing out. And having food and raiment let us be therewith content.
> I Timothy 6: 6–8

While in high school, several things I learned in confirmation class also helped me in my decision making during my high school days. I had always wanted to go to DMLC like my brother did, but that seemed to be out of the question financially for my parents, especially since I had no intention of being a teacher. I also wanted to sing in high school, but, singing in a Christian Day School with all the sacred songs we sang was entirely different than singing anything sacred in a secular school. It was not appropriate for me. The high school choir teacher did not appreciate my Christian version of what to sing or not to sing in his choir, so I did not join the high school choir. As it turned out, when I was in a school talent program as a solo singer, he had to play the piano for me as I sang "The Happy Wanderer."

High school was very good for me in many ways, although I always felt out of place and inferior to others. I did enjoy all the classes, especially my ninth grade English class with Mrs. Sethre as my teacher. She really taught me English grammar which was very useful in my adult writing and editing world. I loved the math classes with Mr. Trandem and enjoyed being in Thespians and doing plays with Mr. Million. I tried out for cheerleading and was so excited to be selected as a B-Squad cheerleader in ninth grade, especially since I was new to public high school as a freshman.

When I was in tenth grade, I was selected as an A-Squad cheerleader. I loved it all! As an A-Squad cheerleader, I was able to do a cartwheel into a full split. Because I could do this, I was one of two on the squad who did this special coach cheer during the third quarter of each game for three years in a row. How special that was for me!

The one thing I especially remember about cheering is that my mother almost always came to our home games and watched me. However, as an A-Squad cheerleader at one game, I was standing by the side of the bleachers during the B-Squad game, just conversing with a couple of people. Suddenly, the side door opened and my mother walked in. She said, "I want to talk to you in the hall." Of course, I followed her out to the hall where she began reprimanding me for "making a spectacle" of myself when I wasn't part of the B-Squad cheerleaders. She told me to go sit in the bleachers and quit "showing off." I felt humiliated as I was not trying to do anything of the kind. But it did teach me to always be aware of where I was and what I was doing in front of others. Thank You, Lord, for the continual guidance of my mother.

In November of 1960, in tenth grade, President Dwight Eisenhower came to our little community to dedicate our new bridge that had replaced the former bridge joining Minnesota to Wisconsin. The town went all out with a parade down the main street which was lined with vendors' stands and food stands. Our high school Latin Club, of which I was a member, had its own food stand with sandwiches all prepared. I made my mom's special minced ham salad filling for the sandwiches I brought. They sold quickly. At last, the president came down the street, riding in an open convertible, and literally sped through town waving to all. Within minutes he had been to the bridge, dedicated it by cutting a ribbon, and then sped back through town again. The bridge was appropriately named the Eisenhower Bridge. We read about it the next day in the *Republican Eagle*, our local newspaper.

Study hall was often a great time for small, quiet conversations while we were studying together. I know at one point I had a conversation with a male classmate of mine, Wayne Madison, for whom I had great respect. I was asking him why I was never asked out to the dances, etc. He said to me very nicely, "You're not the kind of girl a guy wants to date, you're the kind of girl he wants to marry." No one had ever said such a kind, thoughtful, heart-warming thing to me before, and I certainly appreciated it at the time. I have never forgotten it. It was one of the best things that happened in my high school days to give me more confidence at the time. The Lord puts people in your path just when you need them. Thank You, Lord.

In June of 1963, I graduated from Red Wing High School in a class of around two hundred students. I enjoyed all that I did in high school, both the classes and the activities. I was a cheerleader for four years, had been in the Latin Club, Science Club, Discussion Club, GRA (Girls' Recreation Association), and in Thespians in several plays. I was also in the National Honor Society when I graduated. What I didn't know until a couple of years later was that I graduated thirteenth in our class. I have wondered in the past whether if I had known that I was that close to the top ten students, would I have worked any harder on my academics—I think not. As it was, I did get a $250 scholarship at graduation which covered my tuition for my freshman year in college. To God be the glory!

All things work together for good to them that love God,
to them who are the called according to his purpose.
Romans 8:28

Though poor at birth we started life,
Our Lord for us had His plan.
Phil learned the joy of serving God,
Helping out his fellow man.

On Mother's knee I learned to sing,
"Jesus loves me! This I know."
And for my father she would pray
That his Savior God would show.

Chapter 3

Our Courtship

Seek ye first the kingdom of God, and his righteousness;
and all these things will be added unto you.

Matthew 6:33

The time is June 1960, and I had just finished my freshman year in high school. The place is the entry of Our Redeemer's Lutheran Church in Red Wing, Minnesota. My brother, Jim, had attended Dr. Martin Luther High School (DMLC) in New Ulm, Minnesota for three years and had now just graduated high school, in the first graduating class from the newly formed Immanuel Lutheran High School in Mankato, Minnesota. While at DMLC, he would come home on weekends and talk about the new kids from Iowa that had started at DMLC. Since he and I were born in Iowa, it was fun for him to be with these new friends. Jim and I were walking up the inside steps to go into church when the outside doors opened and in walked a group of people. We stopped on the steps and turned around to see who it was. Jim broke into a big smile (He always had an infectious smile!) and greeted them exuberantly. I quickly looked over the group, and my eyes stopped on the face of a boy at the back of the group. He looked tall, even though I was standing on the top step, and had a gentle smile on his face. My brother was talking fast with these people, but I wasn't listening.

"Who is this boy that I see in the back of these people? This is it!" was my first thought. "It's him—the one I have been praying for, over the last ten years. Yes, the Lord has answered my prayers, I know it!" Mom always said, *"Pray without ceasing"* (1 Thessalonians 5:17), as she quoted Scripture so often. There was no doubt whatsoever in my mind about it! Here stood the man of my prayers. I was fifteen years old at the time and had been praying since I was five years old that the Lord would send me a man of my own faith who would be at my side and take me to church every week. And now my prayers had been answered! Here he was! Thank You, Lord!

Then reality set in as my brother began introducing me to this family from Iowa, but I wasn't paying much attention. This boy was still looking at me, eye to eye. I tried to be social and said "Hi" to each one of them. Even to this day I couldn't tell you whom I met. I'm fairly certain this boy's parents were there and a couple of his siblings, but how many and who, by name, were not as clear to me. I didn't want to move as our eyes were still connected and he was looking at me—Jim was introducing this family to me and others in the entry. Their last name was Radichel (pronounced "radical"). Then I heard Jim call the boy's name—Phil. For that moment time stopped and all I could do was thank the Lord again for answering my prayers.

The effectual fervent prayer of a righteous man availeth much.
James 5:16b

The church bell sounded and broke my visual trance. Jim turned back to me, and we went into church and sat down. It was hard focusing on the service that morning. About the only thing I could remember was our eyes meeting and my immediate knowledge that this boy was an answer to prayer.

From his perspective, sometime later Phil told me he noticed me when I was walking down the aisle, probably when church was over and I was going out. He doesn't remember why he noticed—maybe because he thought, "Oh, that's Jim's little sister." He thinks Jim introduced us after church, but he's not sure, probably on the steps outside. But I remember explicitly, it was on the inside steps going into church, and I was on the top step.

Several times during the following year from June 1960—June 1961, when I was a sophomore, I had the chance to see Phil on several different occasions. Our Redeemer's congregation had a youth group that met during the summer for get-togethers. Phil's sister, Lydia, and I became good friends during this time, and we would go to these functions together. Also, my family would go to Mankato for school functions since Jim was there, and I would get to see Phil at some of these outings as well. But as I have said for many years, "It took me a whole year to get a date with him!"

Then in May of 1961, Phil graduated from Immanuel Lutheran High School in Mankato. My brother, Jim, had just finished his freshman year in the college department. After the usual service and graduation ceremonies, I went through with the line of people who were congratulating all the graduates since I knew many of them through Jim. When I came to Phil, I reached out to shake his hand. As he took my hand and our eyes met, he squeezed my hand and didn't let go of it, and I wasn't able—nor did I try—to pull away from his hold on me. It was wonderful! We stood there a while talking until I think we both realized we were holding up the line, but it felt so good just to hold his hand. My heart was beating with such a powerful joy, I don't even remember letting go of his hand—but I must have as others were pushing me on.

Since Phil's parents had moved to Red Wing after his graduation, Phil started working at the Red Wing Pottery while his sister, Lydia, was working there in the office. Both my mother and Shirley had worked there doing hand painting on the dinnerware. Phil worked on the machine that applied the glaze before firing in the kiln. At this time, I was working as a waitress for Lea and "Hutch" Hutchinson at a café in downtown Red Wing.

It was on one of those weekends in June after my sophomore year in high school—a whole year after Phil and I had met—when my brother and I were at our church youth group picnic by Fred Reichert's cabin on the Island. The Island was in the Mississippi River, off the coast of Red Wing, although technically a part of Wisconsin. It was twilight and we were playing Hide and Seek, trying to get back to the fire to say "Free" before we were seen and thus caught by the person who was "it." The game had been called and was over. As I was still leaning over, hiding behind a bush to see if the game was really over, a hand suddenly was laid on my back, and I didn't move. I turned my head slightly to see who it was—it was Phil! I didn't move as he leaned over watching the fire too. Finally, he said, "I think we can go in now. It looks like the game is over." I stood up, and he tenderly took my hand and led me back to the fire. I was unaware that we were still holding hands when we got back to the fire and in front of everyone there. I couldn't tell you what else happened the rest of the night. I had gone to the outing with my brother, Jim, and as we were going home, I said to him, "I'm going to marry Phil." Jim just laughed.

For I know the thoughts that I think toward you,
saith the LORD,
thoughts of peace, and not of evil,
to give you an expected end.
Jeremiah 29:11

It wasn't long after the youth group outing that Phil asked me out on a *real* date—our actual first date! He asked me if I wanted to go see a stock car race at the Red Wing Speedway on the outskirts of Red Wing. Of course, I said "Yes!" if it was with him! I had hurt my wrist somehow earlier in the week and had a removable brace on it. While we were sitting on the bleachers watching the race, he took the brace off my wrist and began massaging my wrist. We ended up spending the night sitting in the bleachers just holding hands. Oh, how great that felt! I do remember someone I knew walking by in front of us while we were holding hands. I was a little embarrassed because I didn't want anyone at school to know I was going with anyone! I can't remember much of anything else about that night except he held my hand and didn't let go of it for most of the night. It didn't hurt at all after that night!

Shortly after the stock car race, Phil invited me to the drive-in movie in Red Wing. Neither one of us remembers what the movie was—that wasn't important. During the evening he had slipped his arm around me and suddenly, we were cheek to cheek. Then, his cheek and mine turned toward each other and our lips met in our first kiss. I was in "seventh heaven" as the saying was in those days. I knew this was the man I had prayed for, and he was in love with me, too. I don't remember much of anything else that night except that first kiss. It was after this special night that we knew we were going to be married, but we also knew that it would be a while before that could happen. I was going to be a junior in high school that fall, and Phil needed to work to be able to go to college.

In December of that year, a friend of ours from church, Conrad Rose, had been talking to Phil and told him he should go to college. Phil said he planned to go but needed to earn some money to do that. Conrad said there was no time like the present and that Phil should just ride up to the Twin Cities with him since it was semester break, and he would show him the campus. Phil went and while he was there he signed up and started winter quarter in January 1962 at the University of Minnesota (U of M).

The next six months were difficult for both of us. During that time Phil found work through the campus employment office for college students. He worked for their inventory department, updating all U of M equipment with new labels and making sure all items were accounted for. Although Phil had saved up money from his days at the Red Wing Pottery, this added money was necessary for food and housing on campus.

Phil didn't come home to Red Wing very often so we would write letters back and forth. If he was home on a weekend, I would write a letter on Sunday night and mail it so he would get it on Tuesday. We would get in a couple of letters each week to each other, noting what we were doing each day. I still have those letters! They show the deepening of our relationship and the growing up of our personalities, especially mine. I was very insecure in high school, and he was instrumental in getting me through it.

During the spring of 1962, the year after Phil's high school graduation, he was invited back to ILC in Mankato for the Spring Banquet. He asked me to go along. I was thrilled! In Red Wing, we had a prom where the main thing was the dance. In Mankato there was no dancing, and the main thing was the meal that was put on by the Junior Class. I was thrilled to be able to go, but I was not sure how to dress. In Red Wing everything was very formal. I asked a few friends who went to ILC for help, and they said I should wear a street length dress. I had a dress from a formal dance I went to in Red Wing so I thought no one in Mankato would have seen it. However, the dress had narrow straps that were to be worn off the shoulder to make it more like a strapless dress. I thought that would be way too risqué for this occasion, so I just pushed the straps up on my shoulders and made it look like a dress with straps. I certainly did not want to look out of place at this dinner. My brother was also at this event since he and two of his buddies were the entertainment for the evening. They played their guitars and sang as the Kingston Trio. We had a great evening.

When Phil's first semester at the U of M was over, he went to work on the farm for his uncle, Herman Levorson, in Northwood, Iowa. He would come home on the weekends, and we would get together at church or at parties. We did maintain a social relationship throughout this time with many of our church friends. During the summertime, we would go to Mankato to visit some of these friends. We went waterskiing on Lake Washington with the Dorings, Klammers, Schweims, and Dryers. Sometimes Phil's brother, Fred, went along with us since he was dating Rosalyn Krueger from Mankato at the time. We made a double date out of it, which was fun.

During August on one of the weekends when Phil was home, we spent time together Sunday afternoon, and it got to be later in the evening than we anticipated. Phil had to leave early in the morning to drive back to Northwood for work. He finally left to go home to get some sleep. The next morning on his way to Iowa, he fell asleep at the wheel, crossed the other lane of traffic, hit a mailbox—which broke the windshield, drove into the ditch just before a field driveway, flew up over that driveway, and nose-dived into the ditch on the other side. Since there were no seatbelts in those days, he hit his nose on the steering wheel and broke it.

When the car stopped and he got his bearings, he found his nose bleeding. He got out of the car and walked to the nearest farmhouse to call for help. We didn't have cell phones in those days. You can imagine the shock of the farmer who opened the door to see this kid with blood running down his face. Phil was taken to Hayfield, Minnesota and saw a doctor who stopped the bleeding and patched him up. A few days later, it was clear that his nose was broken. A doctor in Red Wing fixed his nose by making a splint for it by putting sticks up inside to keep the airway open and filling it with gauze to stop the bleeding. Needless to say, he did not go back to work at his uncle's place for the next month as he recuperated. Of course, there were some comments made about how I had kept him out too late the night before his accident. A few weeks later, after the splint was out, Phil accidentally hit his nose which collapsed it again, and he had to have it reset. After Phil's total recovery from his accident, he decided to take the next school year off and work to get enough money to go back to the U of M in the fall of 1963.

Shortly after that, Phil started work at the Red Wing Shoe Company—working on the actual making of boots. He worked on the second floor of the original factory building in downtown Red Wing. There were times in my senior year in high school that I had evening events or cheerleading practice. When the event was over, or if I left a little early, I would walk down to the Red Wing Shoe Factory to shout up to the open second floor window and call Phil's name. He would lean his head out, cross his arms on the window ledge, and we'd discuss the day. After ten to fifteen minutes, I would head back to the school building a few blocks away and call my dad, who would then come to pick me up. Dad never really knew what I did before he came. Without cell phones, the chance to see and talk with Phil without anyone else knowing was important in our relationship.

While Phil was working at the Red Wing Shoe Factory, he made himself some beautiful boots. He loved those boots and took great care of them. We went bowling on one of our dates and when he got back to the locker room to take off his bowling shoes and put his boots back on, he found that they had been taken. He felt so bad. He really liked those boots. He never found out who took them.

Let him that stole steal no more: but rather let him labour,
working with his hands the thing which is good.
Ephesians 4:28a

One thing my family did a lot as Jim and I were growing up was to go to the lake cabin that my mother's sister, Margaret, and her husband, Carlton Boe, owned on Elbow Lake in northern Minnesota between Park Rapids and Wadena. We would go on weekends after Dad and Mom were done with work on Friday and then come back on Sunday. Mom and I would go out in the boat early in the morning, catch walleye or sun fish, and bring them back to the cabin. Then Dad or Mom would clean the fish and we'd have them for lunch or supper. They tasted so good since they were fresh out of the water. My parents would take Jim and me up there during the summer to help work on the cabin, to go fishing, and to play card games. Years later, after Uncle Boe died, Dad and Mom purchased the cabin from Aunt Marge.

My dear brother Jim and his girlfriend, Carol Lang, started dating about the same time Phil and I did. It was all about church friends and the Lord's hand bringing us all together. God had a purpose for all of us, and He directed our lives so that His purpose would be carried out. The hand of the Lord was easy to watch during our growing-up years, our dating years, our marriages and through the children He gave us to bless our marriages. Yet, we are humbled by what He revealed to us as time went on—the manifestation of His blessings in all of these ways. What if I had done this? Or what if I had not done that? But I don't like to dwell on any of the "what ifs" because it was never in my hands to begin with.

And we know that all things work together for good to them that love God, to them who are the called according to his purpose.
Romans 8:28

While Jim and I were dating Carol and Phil, we would all occasionally get to go to the cabin together with Mom and Dad. At that time there were only two bedrooms and a rollaway bed so the girls would sleep in the extra bedroom and the guys would sleep on the couch and the rollaway out in the main room of the cabin. There was an outhouse and a fish house where they cleaned the fish. We would have so much fun doing many different things there. Sometimes Mom and I would get up early and go fishing for our supper that day. Sometimes we'd be there in the spring, along with Jim and Carol, to put out the dock together or in the fall to bring it back in. The guys would wear bibbed waders to go into the water to lift the dock in order to either put it in or get it out. One of the funniest things I remember was brushing our teeth outside in the morning. We'd each take a paper cup of water and our toothbrush with paste on it and head outside. We would form a line so we could brush and spit, swish some water and spit again until we all had brushed our teeth. Such simple things seemed to make the day much more fun.

At one point while we were at the cabin, Phil even witched a well using two metal coat hangers. He would walk along holding the hangers parallel to each other, and when he crossed the underground stream of water, the hangers would cross each other. Of course, it was hard to believe this was even happening, or was Phil just pretending. But he found several points where the hangers crossed and when they laid out a line on all the points, it appeared to go straight through the garage. At the back side of the garage where the line went, they dug a hole and came up with water. That's where they put the pump to pump the water into the cabin. Wonders never cease!

Through Phil's high school days in Mankato, he developed a strong bond with the Schierenbeck boys, both John and Dave—sons of Pastor L. W. Schierenbeck. Phil learned many things from them, like how to play basketball. John was in Phil's class and was dating a student who was still at DMLC in New Ulm. Our couples relationship grew, and we spent several weekends during those high school days getting together. One weekend John, Phil, and I drove to New Ulm, picked up John's girlfriend, Sharon Huebner, and went to Flandrau State Park. Phil and I had picked up steaks, even though we had little money, and grilled those steaks in the park. What made it so special is the close bond between us as Christian couples, sharing our wealth and enjoying each other's company. Those are some of the best memories we share of our dating lives.

I enjoyed so many wonderful friendships that I gathered while at Red Wing High School, many of which have lasted a lifetime. Our class started having class reunions in our tenth year after graduation. We have had them consistently since then at five- or ten-year intervals. I have been fortunate to be part of the planning team almost since the beginning. I do love memories. I will say though, it took me ten to fifteen years after high school to get over the inferiority complex I had developed in high school. I didn't feel I could compete personally with several of my friends. It took my husband many years to get me through those thoughts. But the Lord continued to work in me as He gave me more work to do in His kingdom. This work included bringing up the blessings He gave us later in our married life.

In the fall of 1963, I began my college days at the U of M, where Phil was as well. The first year I tried living in a rooming house off campus and walking to school each day. My roommate was Jan Lorenz. I don't remember how we met, but we hit it off right away. Sometimes when I'd go home on weekends, I'd bake several dozen chocolate chip cookies and bring a full shoebox back to school that Jan and I would share. Phil would get a few of those as well. After the first quarter, Jan and I moved into Powell Hall on campus by the U of M Hospital since I was going to be a medical technologist and would have many classes in the hospital area. Powell Hall was a "no food" girls' dorm so we had to eat at the cafeteria if we wanted to eat. Jan was my roommate for the two and a half years I lived there. We got to be such great friends that she was a bridesmaid at our wedding.

Phil and I would drive to our homes in Red Wing most weekends so we could eat. That's when I would make those cookies by the boxful and bring them back. Some great talking time happened on those trips, while a few off-road stops were made. On one of those off-road stops, we got so stuck in the mud we had to use the car jack to lift the front end of the car and then step on the gas and push the car at the same time to eventually get out of the mud.

At this time Phil lived off campus by Memorial Stadium in a rooming house. While he lived there, his friend, Jim Reim, came to visit him for a while and ended up sleeping on the floor of his room until the dorm supervisor told Phil that Jim had to leave. Phil signed a bank note so Jim could get a car. Jim slept in that car for a while just to have a place to sleep.

Of course, I needed to work to help pay my bills, and I really appreciated the jump start of my high school scholarship. I found work in the research lab of Dr. Rodney Harvey who was doing research on the kidney while using dogs as his subjects. His assistant was a med tech named Joan with whom I got along well. I was the dishwasher and the lab assistant to Joan. We washed all dishes and surgical equipment by hand and let them air dry.

There are a couple of major events which I remember vividly that happened while I worked in Dr. Harvey's lab. The first one occurred on Friday, Nov 22, 1963. I was standing at the sink washing dishes as usual when Dr. Harvey walked in the door, his face white as a sheet. He looked at me and said words I will never forget, "Some ********* fool shot the president. Go home, we're done here!" I left the lab and went back to Coffman Union where everyone was gathering around the one or two TVs in the main ballroom watching this major event in our country unfold—the assassination of President John F. Kennedy. I ran into Phil who had also been watching it, and we got our things ready and drove back to Red Wing to spend the weekend separately with each set of our parents. On Sunday, November 24, I was alone in the house watching all the news on TV when Jack Ruby forced his way between the journalists and cameramen and shot Lee Harvey Oswald, the accused killer of the president. All of this was live on TV as was the actual shooting of the president in the motorcade as they were proceeding down the main street of Dallas at the time. These events flood my memory all over again each time I drive by the memorial square in Dallas.

The other event I think of in Dr. Harvey's office occurred when I was angry over something that happened in the lab. What happened I don't remember, but I think I was reprimanded for something that I didn't feel I deserved. I was washing a huge glass flask at the time and swishing the water around in it when it just barely touched the edge of the sink and shattered, cutting my finger quite badly. Of course, I dropped the flask and turned the water on to wash the blood away as Dr. Harvey came by. I said in somewhat of an angry voice, "I'm going to ER. I'll finish this when I get back." I got a clean towel, put lots of pressure on my ring finger and headed toward the ER. I then remembered that it was only one year until the day that Phil and I were to be married and I wasn't sure how my hand would heal. It was my ring finger, but at least not the one on my left hand.

Phil and I often pooled our money to pay a tuition bill or buy supper. To economize and share expenses, we often ate lunch at Coffman Union's cafeteria. We would get the lunch plate of the day—a hamburger with fries and lettuce and a tomato on the side for about fifty cents. We'd put the lettuce and tomato on the hamburger, cut it in half so we each could have a half of the hamburger and then split the fries. That was usually our lunch and sometimes also our breakfast or supper. But we were happy and content with it. Thank You, Lord, for providing food and raiment at a time when we had little.

As the next semester was rolling around, times were getting tight and lunch money was sparse. One weekend trip home I asked Dad and Mom if I could have $500 to help with food and tuition that year. The answer was NO! They were paying for Jim's schooling already. I also remember they still bowled two times each during the week and both smoked two packs of cigarettes a day. There was always bourbon in the house for them when they wanted it. I remember thinking that when I had kids, I would try anything to help them with schooling. At the same time, it taught me to save more and spend less on extras. Later, after we were married, we did ask Jim and Carol, who were also married and both working, if we could borrow some money for expenses, and they gave it to us. Thank You, Lord!

Phil and I dated for five years before we decided to get married. We always assumed we would get married, so there was never any official proposal event. I really didn't think one should marry anyway before they were twenty-one. But as I continued to watch the hand of the Lord, He was giving us this time to really grow up as a couple and learn to understand each other's personality better.

And having food and raiment let us be therewith content.
I Timothy 6:8

Seeking first our God's righteousness
While knowing He cares for us,
When we watch His hand in our lives,
We have so much to discuss.

The relationship we cherished
With our Father up above,
Brought our pathways close together
Helping to mature our love.

Chapter 4

Our Marriage

What therefore God hath joined together,
let not man put asunder.

Matthew 19:6

The Place:

> On the terraces of *Sandy Acres*, Red Wing, Minnesota,
> August 6, 1966

The People:

> **Ministers:** Brother Jim performed the wedding vows;
>   Pastor George Barthels gave the sermonette
> **Best Man:** John Schierenbeck
> **Groomsmen:** Frank Radichel, Fred Radichel, Gary Hayden
> **Maid of Honor:** Lydia Radichel
> **Bridesmaids:** Sandy Stuber, Sharla Watermolen, Jan Lorenz
> **Ring Bearers:** Jon Heath (my godchild) and Tom Lentz
>   (Phil's godchild)
> **Flower Girl:** Beth Markgraf (Phil's niece)
> **Ushers:** Jim Reim, Fred Reichert

Photographer: Conrad Rose
Organist: Veva Stehr
Soloist: Alvin Sieg
Personal Attendant: Carol Sandeen
Gift Openers: Lois Barthels and Sharon Huebner
Punch Server: Gwen Ellingson
Coffee Server: Aunt Martha Levorson
Cake Server: Aunt Gerane Fannon

On our wedding day, although the forecast was for rain, the sky was a clear, beautiful blue and the sun was shining brightly. In the morning Dad (Gilbert) Radichel came to build the kneeling rail and place the pillow on it. He then put it on the second terrace by the flat stones that Mom (Ann) Sandeen had built for this purpose with steps

I loved all the white against the green of the trees and hills.

leading up to it. There was enough room for the kneeling bench and for us to stand in front of it along with enough room for the minister to stand behind it. We had placed two folding chairs toward the back of the terrace for the ministers to sit when they were not participating. Gwen and Waldo Johnson had sent potted flowers that morning which we put at the bottom of the stairs. After all the groundwork was done over the few years before our wedding, the yard was lush and beautiful. We had borrowed chairs from church, and they were all set up facing the terrace. Dad brought his Hammond organ out of the house and left it on the front sidewalk. On the other side of the garage, Mom and Dad had built a fishpond into the side of the terrace. For this occasion, Mom had added goldfish to the pond and surrounded the terrace side with flowers. It was truly beautiful.

Before the service, Gary Hayden had taken our 1957 pink Plymouth and parked it downtown so people wouldn't find it and try to decorate or mess with it. We were afraid the car wouldn't hold up to anything anyone would try to do to it. After the service and reception, Gary chauffeured us back to our car so we could leave for our honeymoon.

I had such a good time at Jim and Carol's wedding just eight weeks earlier helping Carol get ready that I could hardly wait for her to help me. We dressed in Mom and Dad's bedroom upstairs in our house and could watch what was going on in the front yard from the window. We could see who was coming and where people were sitting. After some private talk, we left the room, and Conrad Rose came in to take wedding pictures from that same window.

Jon Heath caught his heel in his bike spokes earlier that week and tore some skin so he was not able to wear shoes that day. With his black socks on and his black tuxedo pants, you couldn't tell he wasn't wearing shoes. However, our yard had lots of stickle burrs, so he did have trouble walking down the aisle. As a six-year-old, he did quite

Tom, Beth, and Jon brought fun
and joy to our wedding.

well holding his ring pillow straight and trying not to worry about his feet being poked with the stickle burrs. What a trooper!

Tom Lentz's mother was quite upset that the suit we got for him to wear had not been tried on before our wedding day. It was a tad too big for him, but he wore it well and was as handsome as ever. Tom, at three years old, was the epitome of a mature ring bearer. As he began to walk around the side of the house to go down the main aisle, he kept hitting his one fist into the palm of his other fist saying to himself, "I'm not going to do this!" He was so like his Uncle Phil would have been if he had been required to do this same thing.

Beth Markgraf, also three years old, was adorable in her all-white long dress and her wispy short white veil pinned in her hair, carrying a little basket of rose petals. She made it all the way up to her spot on the first step until a fly got caught under her veil. She then retreated to her mother and stayed with her the rest of the service after a job well done.

The service started right on time at 2:00 p.m. Dad met me outside the porch door by the driveway. After giving me a hug, we started down the sidewalk following my beautiful bridesmaids, the handsome ring bearers, and our adorable flower girl as she began to sprinkle rose petals in front of me. As we turned to the front of the house and down the grassy aisle to the terraces with Veva playing beautiful music, such as "Sheep May Safely Graze," my eyes met the eyes of the man the Lord had given to me, now standing at the bottom of the steps. He looked so handsome in his white tuxedo jacket with black pants. He was surrounded by his groomsmen in their white coats with black pants and the bridesmaids in their all-white matching dresses with short, white veil headpieces. What a glorious day the Lord was giving us.

During the service, Pastor George Barthels delivered the address while my dear brother Jim, now just one month into his ministry, proceeded with our marriage vows and pronounced us husband and wife in the name of our Triune God—Father, Son, and Holy Ghost. Surely God had led us to this moment in time to bring us together for His purpose. We were ready for it. He had been with us these last six years we had known each other, five years since we both acknowledged we were meant to be together in this life. Thank You, Lord, for the many blessings you have shown us through the fifty-six years of our lives together. My confirmation Bible verse came back to me, *"But seek ye first the kingdom of God, and his righteousness; and all these things shall be added unto you"* (Matthew 6:33).

As we turned and walked down the stone steps, we led the procession around the front of the house to the back where we gathered the receiving line in front of the fishpond with real goldfish. The flowers and bushes were in full bloom. As the people came by to greet us, they walked toward the garage where Gwen served the punch and continued around the back of the house to pick up their sandwiches and cake. Then they went back toward the chairs where they had been sitting for the service to eat. This circling of the house continued until everyone was back in their seats.

Phil and I proceeded into the garage which had been decorated with crepe paper the night before. Those decorations had absorbed the moisture of the night and had been hanging almost to the floor the morning of the wedding. Mom said to just give it time and they would tighten back up again. She was right and by noon all was well with the decorations. We had set up tables from church to put the gifts on as Lois and Sharon opened them all for us so everyone could see what we had received. Over the years the practice of someone else opening gifts has dwindled while the joy of opening your own gifts has taken precedence for the bride and groom.

Every good gift and every perfect gift is from above,
and cometh down from the Father of lights.
James 1:17a

Around 4:00 p.m., after changing into our traveling clothes, Phil and I bid our parents and family goodbye and had our chauffeur take us to our car downtown. We headed for supper at the Afton House just upriver from Red Wing. We weren't out of town for more than a few minutes, and we could see the forecasted rain clouds coming in from the west. Mom later said that we were gone about a half hour when the rain hit. Everyone who was still there headed for the garage, and they partied on!

After a very special lobster meal at the Afton House, we continued to St. Paul for our honeymoon night at the Ramada Inn on Hwy 94. As we were getting ready for bed, Phil asked me if I had brushed my teeth. It's not one of those things you would expect a new groom to ask his bride before bed, and I was taken aback by the question. I asked him "Why?" I will never forget his response, "If you want to go to bed with me, you will need to brush your teeth." I hadn't brushed my teeth before bed much at all when I was growing up; however, I have seldom missed a night since! I thought of those words almost every time we drove past that hotel in the years to follow. Even now, years after the hotel was torn down, I often think of it driving past the site. The husband is the head of the house.

The next day we journeyed upriver to a beautiful camp site on the Mississippi River. We bought a rick of wood at a local gas station and headed for our site. We got the camp set up just before the rain started. Thanks to Phil's sister, Margaret, and her husband, Ray, we had borrowed their tent along with two twin size mattress pads and two twin sleeping bags. We opened the bottle of champagne that was given to us as a wedding gift and drank it from the hollow stemmed glasses that came with the champagne as the rain poured down outside the tent. That night we pushed the two mattresses together side by side, opened one of the sleeping bags to put on top of the pads, and used the other sleeping bag as a cover. We didn't get much sleep that night though. Every time we tried to move toward each other, the two mattress pads would slide apart, and we'd be on the ground. After a few hours, I think, we just ended up sleeping on the ground— it was easier. When we finally woke up the next day, we saw the snaps on the side of each mattress pad that should have been snapped to hold the pads together. Should we ever camp in a tent again, I'm sure we won't make the same mistake! Thank You, Lord, for the blessing of this man You gave me.

> *The husband is the head of the wife,*
> *even as Christ is the head of the church.*
> Ephesians 5:23

This passage has been one of the principles of doctrine that has always been a staple for me. This principle was evident in my growing up years even before my father became a Christian. He and Mom always discussed important things before they acted on them. I don't really remember any time when Mom just did what she wanted on anything important regardless of what Dad said. But then I was not always around or privy to their discussions. What I do remember is Dad's focus on our spiritual training after he found his Lord and worked for the continuation of our church. He never turned back from his duty to take charge of the family and see that each person continued in the way of the Lord.

My pastor through my grade school years, Pastor George Barthels, was very thorough in his explanation of God's plan for the family starting with Adam and Eve. I knew my place as a spouse and what's more, my husband knew his place as my husband but never lorded it over me. Instead, he has always listened to what I have said and weighed it in the balance of his decision. We continually thank our Lord for His guidance in our relationship. And now, more than sixty years later, we are as much or more blessed in our personal relationship with respect for each other. To God be the glory!

Our first apartment after we were married was at 615 University Avenue, a short distance from the University of Minnesota (U of M). Our unit was on the upper level of a two-story home that had four apartments on the upper level, each comprising one-fourth of the upstairs. This unit was considered an efficiency apartment as it had basically one large room that was partially divided into a large living room and a large kitchen-dining room. This large area pretty much made up the whole apartment. There was also a small bathroom by the entry and an enclosed porch off the living room that you entered through French doors. The porch had windows all around it. We liked to say the porch hung out toward the street and big trucks going by would rattle the porch. However, we still used that enclosed porch as our bedroom during the warmer months of August through December and then again from April through the summer. During the cold months, we brought the bed into the living room.

Since we were beginning our senior year at the U of M and still had lots of studying to do, Phil bought a 4' x 8' sheet of plywood and some concrete blocks. We made a huge desk that sat in the middle of our living room. Bookcases were made by using boards between the blocks on each end of the desk. That lasted for two years until we moved.

Our other furniture included a spool couch that came from Phil's folks, so we had a place for people to sit, and a folding table that came from Vera and Bell's trailer along with some folding chairs. There was one small dresser that we used to keep some clothes in and a small closet by the bathroom for hanging clothes. We were content.

And having food and raiment let us be therewith content.
I Timothy 6:8

When I think of that first year after we were married, I remember how great it was to be in our small apartment and be only a few blocks from the U of M. We could walk to classes if we wanted to and not worry about parking, or we could drive and park in the river lot and walk up the hill to classes. We borrowed money for our final year in college through the Federal Government Student Loan Program. I couldn't work during that year since my whole school year was learning in the University Hospital laboratory doing actual lab work.

Phil and I would still occasionally drive home on weekends to eat at our parents' homes, and sometimes bring food from them back to our home. When we stayed in town, we would go to our new church home at Grace Lutheran Church in Fridley, Minnesota. We had gone to Grace occasionally during our first years at the U of M as well as to Berea Lutheran when they were on University Avenue in St. Paul. Berea eventually bought land and built a church in Inver Grove Heights, south of St. Paul, which was much further away from the U of M. Grace was a small church/parsonage building built in 1958. We have remained members there since joining in 1966.

In May of 1967, both Phil and I graduated from the U of M. Phil graduated with a degree in Electrical Engineering from the Institute of Technology, while I graduated with a degree in Medical Technology. Our commencement exercises were in the U of M football stadium with all graduates of that year. We each sat with our individual schools and walked up one by one to receive our postcard to be sent back to the administration to have our diploma sent to us.

Graduation took a few hours but was a beautiful day. Later Verona and Ed Lentz had a graduation get-together at their home in New Hope, Minnesota. Thank You, Lord, for getting us through those lean years of hard work and preparing us for what You would have us do in our future lives.

Phil's last job during college started after we were married. Since he had been in the Institute of Technology, he went to a college fair on campus where employers would come to campus and look for interns for the summer. He signed up for his summer job with Honeywell, Inc. in New Brighton, Minnesota. After graduating, he interviewed with several companies in town as well as Martin Marietta from Colorado, but since we didn't have a church near the Colorado company, he chose to stay at Honeywell in Minneapolis designing test equipment. It was said at that time, "Once a Honeywell man, always a Honeywell man." He ended up working for them for almost thirty years.

I continued working at North Memorial Hospital in Robbinsdale, Minnesota, but now as a full-time medical technologist. We each enjoyed our new positions. Since we had only one car, Phil dropped me off in downtown Minneapolis at 6:00 a.m. so I could catch a bus to Robbinsdale while he then continued to Hopkins. We moved after a year of this, in 1968.

Our new apartment was on Douglas Drive in Golden Valley in a real apartment complex. We were on the second floor in a two-bedroom apartment. We even had our own single-car garage. It was fun to decorate this new place. We turned that 4' x 8' sheet of plywood that Phil had purchased for our desk in the first apartment into a sewing table for me and used the second bedroom for it. There I made most of my clothes, including my lab dresses.

About four blocks away from this apartment was a new Byerly's grocery store. We would often stop there on the way home from work and grab supper to take home. They had, and still have, delicious food to go which I appreciated since I wasn't the greatest cook. My brother, Jim, was always the one to do the cooking when we spent summers at home while our parents were working.

We enjoyed having family and friends visit, as they were able, and would invite our minister from Grace and his family, Pastor and Mrs. Carl Thurow, for dinner occasionally. My mother had always told me that we should always look out for our pastor as he was God's spiritual gift to us. In Red Wing she used to invite Pastor Barthels and his entire family, ten people, for Sunday dinner after church once a month. I will always remember how much joy it gave her to serve them.

Phil had moved his work at Honeywell from Hopkins to the St. Louis Park plant for more workspace and because it was closer to home. He was working on a special test equipment project for the government which needed to be done. Once he had been working long hours during a one-week timeframe, with little or no sleep and not even coming home. During one of those long nights, things weren't going well so he said he stopped for a moment and said a prayer. Things got better! Thank You, dear Lord! As it turned out, I had booked us on a plane for a getaway to Spokane, Washington, where our friends, Pastor John and Sharon Schierenbeck were living. They had just had a new baby, Jeff, and I wanted to go out to see them and Phil needed the time off. On that Friday morning, I waited for an hour or more outside the door of Honeywell to pick Phil up to go to the airport. I called a couple of times to see when he would be done so we could catch our plane. We did finally make it to the airport in time for our flight. When we reached Spokane and got to John and Sharon's house, I put Phil to bed in a quiet bedroom downstairs. He spent most of the weekend sleeping, unless we woke him to eat and go to the bathroom. Otherwise, he finally got up for church on Sunday morning. After lunch and a quick card game, we left for the airport and home. Thank You again, Lord, for dear friends, rest, and our safe journey.

With God all things are possible.
Matthew 19:26b

After I worked full time at North Memorial Hospital for a while, I was asked to be assistant hematology tech. I did love the hematology department. I was very good at doing venipunctures and would be the one they would send to the floor when a tech couldn't find a vein to draw the blood we needed for testing. I was even able to do newborn babies and did a scalp vein at one time to get blood for the test the doctor needed. I also loved using the laboratory equipment and would troubleshoot a few if there were problems.

During this time the hospital administration was considering a full-time dedicated computer for the laboratory. Our chief pathologist, Dr. Semba, wanted to have the ability to get lab results back to the floors as soon as possible so the doctors would be able to treat patients more quickly. He wanted to set up individual workstations on a computer to record results from the equipment and enter them into the mainframe. The nurses' stations on the floors could then receive their patient results immediately. I was asked to be the laboratory assistant chief technologist under our chief tech Jean Speck. I would help Mrs. Speck with a lot of different administrative work, including setting up the worker schedules in each lab department for the week, making sure all departments were fully covered with lab techs, medical lab assistants, etc. We had separate departments for blood bank, urology, hematology, chemistry, bacteriology, and EKG. Depending on the education of each lab person, all departments had different requirements for each part of the work they did. The work schedule was a major part of my duties—until the new computer mainframe joined the laboratory. Then the work was really involved, and I loved it!

I was responsible for working with the computer installation company in organizing the different department terminals, training the staff in how to use them, and troubleshooting when there were errors before calling for help from the computer company. This was the second computerized laboratory in the metropolitan area of Minneapolis and St. Paul. Hennepin County General Hospital had been the first. As a regional hospital for the state of Minnesota, North Memorial Hospital was very proud of this accomplishment.

One of the most memorable events of my medical technology career occurred during a severe thunderstorm we had shortly after our computer was installed. During the night a lightning bolt caused a power outage in the hospital. When the emergency power came back on, our lab computer didn't. The computer company was called to get it restarted with a separate power generator. Meanwhile, Dr. Semba and I were working to get patient results out the old way. After the morning rush of patient information going to the floors, we were ready to start putting in the data. I started up the computer, entering the date and other pertinent information. We then worked for a number of hours getting all the data back into the computer manually. At the end of that time, we tried to download the information to store it and were not able to do that. We looked back on the paper trail of all the work we had done, and I realized I had entered the wrong date at the very beginning of our work, many hours earlier. I put my head down on the terminal and was ready to cry. Dr. Semba came over to me, put his hand on my shoulder, and said not to worry. He said we should be pretty good by now in knowing how to get the data in without any trouble. So, I had someone else enter the date! We took a coffee break and started again to manually enter the data. Dr. Semba was right, it didn't take us nearly as long to do it the second time, and we got it done!

The years after our wedding and before we had children allowed us to spend a lot of free time with family and friends. We often got together with Jim and Carol. They had started off their marriage in Millston, Wisconsin, and we would drive down there for a weekend. Millston was about sixty-five miles south of Eau Claire. We were not only siblings to one another, but great friends. Carol told me at one point a number of years ago that she thought the best thing about coming into our family was the "huggy, loving arms" acceptance that wasn't part of her upbringing. She said that our mom always made her feel that she was accepted for what and who she was and didn't expect Carol to change just because she was part of the family. Mom wasn't possessive of Jim either and let him do as he wanted. To Carol, Dad was always the teddy bear—sweet and loving, a fine Christian man. Carol liked to say about Dad that *there is joy in heaven over one sinner that repents* (cf Luke 15:7).

While Jim and Carol lived in Millston, we took a fun trip down to see them with John and Sharon Schierenbeck after they were married in the fall of 1966. We did some hiking in the area and at one point we were going to climb a fire ranger tower. John did not like heights of any kind and couldn't get up more than a couple of steps and had to have help getting down. Several years later we managed to get John on a gondola and had him close his eyes to get to the other side of the ride. We did enjoy each other's company as good Christian friends.

A few years later, Jim took a ministerial call to Marquette, Michigan. Phil and I drove to Millston to help load the truck. After that we loved to go visit them in Marquette as the drive was beautiful. One of Carol's favorite stories about Marquette was about the cat they had at the time. Phil was not fond of cats at all. When we got there on one trip and Phil opened the door into their kitchen, the cat was on top of the refrigerator by the door. As soon as Phil walked by the refrigerator, the cat jumped out on Phil's head and surprised him. Phil was not a happy camper but only booted the cat away. He stayed far away from the cat after that incident.

We often went to the Elbow Lake cabin in the summers. Since Phil and I had graduated from college and were actually making some money, we went to the Minneapolis Boat Show to dream about our future. We found a "Do It Yourself" kit to make a pontoon boat that wasn't very expensive. We thought how fun it would be to have a pontoon at the lake. We could use it as a swimming dock, pushing off the shoreline and anchoring it in deeper water. Or we could take it out as a family, and some of us could fish while the others could sit on chairs and enjoy the great outdoors. So, we bought enough pontoons to build one. They were light weight and came with canned ingredients to fill each plastic pontoon in order to give them greater floating capability. How excited we were. We arranged with Jim and Carol to be there the same weekend we were so Phil and Jim could do this together. Without reading the directions completely, they took a bucket and mixed Part A and Part B together so they could then pour the contents into each pontoon. The part they missed by not reading the directions was that you should mix the parts within the pontoon as the mixture immediately expanded and overflowed the bucket and then began to harden. The guys laughed over their mistake and started over again, correctly filling the remaining pontoons. When they had the deck built and the pontoons added, we all had great fun for years to come.

If any would not work, neither should he eat.
2 Thessalonians 3:10b

Oh, the joy of Your rich blessings
As we join as man and wife.
May You always keep us faithful
To Your Word throughout our life.

For the work that You've allowed us,
For Your grace along our way,
You have giv'n us rich abundance
And we thank You every day.

Chapter 5

Our Early Family Life

And, ye fathers, provoke not your children to wrath:
but bring them up in the nurture and admonition of the Lord.

Ephesians 6:4

During the five years we dated, Phil and I often talked about having children—how many, male or female, how we would raise them, etc. I would imagine most people who know they are getting married discuss a family and if/when they want to start one. We had talked about waiting a few years after we were married, since we would just be graduating from college, and I wanted to work a while to use the education I earned. I wanted to be home with our children unlike my mother who was not at home with my brother and me when we were young.

People getting married may even discuss where they want their children to go to school or church (especially if the couple is from two different religious backgrounds). This is one of the main reasons I had always prayed for a man of my own faith so that there would never be a question as to where we would go to church or about the spiritual training of our children. The Lord has richly blessed us in this regard. We felt the spiritual discipline from both parents was a vital need for a child, especially in their first five years, so we chose to keep our children at home until kindergarten with no formal preschool. In addition, we felt that the choice for Christian education was too important to be left in a child's hands, so we chose to send our children to a Christian Day School. Such biblical references as *"He that spareth his rod hateth his son: but he that loveth him chasteneth him betimes"* (Proverbs 13:24) and *"Train up a child in the way he should go: and when he is old, he will not depart from it"* (Proverbs 22:6) are commandments the Lord gave to all parents to help preserve and protect the child from straying and following the world's ways.

In talking about the number of children we wanted to have, we used our own family situations for examples. Phil had been one of seven children while I was one of two children in our immediate family. Of course, I had Shirley whom I loved as a sister, but she was nine years older than I was and often spent her summers in Iowa. She wasn't around when Jim and I were roaming the hills. I also had Charlie and Doris who were not around much at all and they were also much older than I was. So, Phil and I decided that four children would be about right, God willing.

I also appreciated the male headship example I had growing up in that my older brother, Jim, was always ready to take charge of what happened in our days together. He would decide if what we did was appropriate for me or was safe for me. I always looked up to him and trusted his advice or decisions. Phil and I wanted that type of male leadership example for our children as well and even went so far as to go through a book we found in the library called *How to Determine the Sex of Your Baby*. And yes, we did go through the steps involved and by God's plan our firstborn was indeed a boy, while the second child was a girl. I was feeling so blessed with this structure of our family, although I'm not sure the example meant quite as much to these two siblings as it did to me.

We only stayed in the apartment on Douglas Drive in Golden Valley for two years and in 1970 we moved into a brand-new apartment complex called Oregon Estates off 42nd Avenue in New Hope, a few miles north of Golden Valley. It was nice to be the first ones in a newly built apartment. We were on the second floor and had a balcony. The unit also came with a single car garage stall. We were only there a year, but I continued to use that plywood piece we bought in college as a sewing table, still making my uniforms and church clothes. A year later we bought a lot in a new community in New Hope. We picked the split entry house plan we liked for the walkout lot and moved into 3213 Gettysburg Avenue in the fall of 1971.

That Christmas in 1971 was indeed a memorable one. We did not go to any other family member's home, nor did anyone come to our home that year. I was eight months pregnant with our first child. But we had lots of presents under the tree. I had a great time at hardware stores buying my husband all kinds of tools since we were going to finish off the unfinished walkout basement ourselves to complete our home. We also purchased baby furniture and baby clothes and put those items under the tree. After the Christmas Eve service at church, as was each of our customs growing up, we spent the rest of the evening opening each gift. So, our first Christmas in our own home was also our last Christmas alone.

Toward the end of January, while I was at work, Phil called me to say that he was going to be late in picking me up. Since I was now nine months pregnant and tired from working all day, I went into the EKG room after my shift and laid down to rest on the EKG bed. When Phil got there, he asked me if I felt like I was having any labor pains and wanted to stay at the hospital or go home. We were having a snowstorm at the time. I said I was doing okay so we went home. Later that night I couldn't sleep much and by early morning we decided I needed to go to the hospital. It had been snowing all night and when Phil backed out of the garage and started up the street, he got stuck in the snow and couldn't go any further. Phil then got out of the car and told me to get behind the wheel and he would try to push us out of the drift. So, I wiggled my way behind the steering wheel and tried to steer while Phil tried to push the car. When that didn't work, Plan B went into action.

Phil went back into the house and called the police to tell them we needed help and why. Within minutes a police officer was there and when he saw me behind the wheel, he just shook his head at me. He told Phil that a snowplow was on the way. As soon as he said that, we saw the plow go across the street in front of us, it went around the block and came behind us, and literally pushed us up to where he had already plowed. The officer told us that an ambulance was on its way and would be there shortly. Phil said we were just going to drive to the hospital. After we got up to the main street, we saw the lights of the ambulance. I told Phil I wasn't going to *my* hospital in an ambulance. Phil said there was no way we would be able to flag down the ambulance anyway, so he just drove on. Since it was early in the morning, Phil drove a little faster than the speed limit and as we pulled into the emergency entrance to North Memorial Hospital, the ambulance pulled in behind us. They got a wheelchair for me and sent Phil to the admitting department while they took me up to the delivery room.

On Tuesday, January 25, 1972, at 10:38 a.m., our first gift from God, Brian David Radichel, was born. He weighed 8 lb. 11 oz. and was 21" long. His head measured 13.25" around and his chest was 13.5". What a joy it was to have a son to carry on the Radichel name. Since we had discussed the importance of baptism and all that goes with it ahead of time, we had asked Phil's sister, Verona, and her husband, Ed Lentz, to be the godparents of our son. We also wanted to have our children baptized as soon as we could after they were born. That was very important to both of us. On Friday, January 28, because our Pastor H. C. Duehlmeier was not available at the time, we called Pastor Paul

Larsen from our sister congregation, Berea, in Inver Grove Heights, who came to the hospital for Brian's baptism. Thank You, Lord, for Your saving grace through baptism. We have prayed continually for Brian that he would remain faithful throughout his life.

I went back to work at North Memorial Hospital shortly after Brian was born and continued to work; but it was the second shift every other weekend (Friday through Sunday) 3:00 p.m.—11:00 p.m. instead of working during the week. That way I was still able to go to church Sunday morning and be with my new baby at night. There was a family in our neighborhood that had two teenage girls who helped me on Fridays. One of them got off school around 2:00 p.m. and came right to our house to stay with Brian while I went to work. Phil would get home before 5:00 p.m. so the sitter could go home, and he would have Brian through supper and until I got home at 11:30 p.m. This worked out well.

Phil's sister, Verona, told me when I was pregnant with Brian, "Take this child with you wherever you go now. It only gets harder when you have more children." Yes, in fact, I did that a lot. We even drove to Seattle with him when he was less than a year old. We put him in the back seat of our two-door yellow Capri when we went out to Washington to see Bob and Aunt Janey (Dad's sister, Gerane) Reed. Phil had made a plywood board to fit the whole back seat of our car with legs on the front end of the board and a pillow under the back end of the board by the seat back in order to balance it. I covered it with a heavy blanket. Brian slept or played on that board the entire trip. I could get up, turn around, and change his diaper there too. Those were the days of no seat belt laws. At the same time, it was very dangerous because Brian could be thrown around in the car if we had an accident. After that trip, I decided I would never have anything but a four-door car anymore. If we would have had an accident or any kind of emergency, we couldn't have opened a back door to get him out very easily. Thank You, Lord, for protecting our baby during the entire trip!

We had decided earlier that we wanted our second child, preferably a girl, close in age to Brian so they could be friends and be able to play together and be close in school together. On Saturday, May 19, 1973, at 2:47 p.m., our second gift from God, Tina Jean Radichel, was born. She weighed 7 lbs. 12.25 oz. and was 20" long. Her head measured 13.5" and her chest was 13.5". The next day, Sunday, May 20, Pastor H. C. Duehlmeier came to the hospital and baptized Tina. Thank You, Lord, for giving Your saving grace through baptism and Your Word. Uncle Ed and Auntie Verona Lentz were also Tina's godparents. We wanted the same godparents in case anything should happen to Phil and me, they would see to it that our children would be brought up *"in the nurture and admonition of the Lord"* (Ephesians 6:4).

After our first two children were born, I was still working the night shift so I could be their caregiver during the day. Phil and I were thinking maybe two children would be enough. We decided we would still take precautions but continue to leave the whole subject of more children in the Lord's hands, which we knew had been the case all along anyway. By the time Tina was one and a half, I decided to quit work all together to be with both children all the time. This also gave us more time to work-in our family devotions at mealtime, and I could sing to the children each night at bedtime when they said their prayers. Or as the Lord said, *"Train up a child in the way he should go: and when he is old, he will not depart from it"* (Proverbs 22:6).

At last Brian was five and ready for kindergarten. I had my hands full with caring for the children and keeping the house. We had also completed the work on the lower level of the house so both Brian and Tina had their own bedrooms on the main floor. Phil and I had our bedroom and an office in the lower level. I used that office as my sewing room. However, instead of the ten-year-old piece of plywood from our college days, we stained and varnished an old door which made a beautiful table. I continued to make most of my clothes as well as our family dress clothes for church. I made matching leisure suits for Phil and Brian along with pretty dresses for Tina.

In the fall of 1977, Brian started kindergarten at Sonnesyn Elementary School in New Hope. His teacher was Mrs. Janet Parker, a woman I dearly loved and appreciated for all she did for Brian in his first year of school. We have kept in touch with her ever since. Brian walked to school each day the weather was good. In the winter, I took him. He had other neighborhood friends from school that he would walk with occasionally.

One of the classmates Brian occasionally walked with was a little girl who was Jewish. One day Brian came home from school and told me what he and this little girl had talked about. He brought up something about church and Jesus. He asked her if she believed in Jesus and when she said she didn't, he said to her, "You're going to hell!" I couldn't believe what he actually said to her, but he did know that Jesus was the way to salvation. I wondered if I was going to get a phone call from this little girl's parents, but never did.

Out of the mouth of babes!
Psalm 8:2

Five years after Tina was born the Lord decided it was time for our third child. My parents were in the process of retiring, not just from work, but from Red Wing itself. They had decided to move north, up by Elbow Lake, so they could go back and forth to the cabin any time they wanted. Since we had a CLC congregation in Detroit Lakes, Minnesota, they bought property in that community and were in the process of building a house. We used their fortieth wedding anniversary on May 1, 1978, as an appropriate time to celebrate the Ruby Anniversary and have a retirement party at the same time. We put a notice in the Red Wing Republican Eagle newspaper regarding the party we were having at Our Redeemer's Church in Red Wing, and we expected to have many people at the reception.

Since I had become a cake decorator as well as a seamstress, I decided to make their three-tiered anniversary cake myself. Jim and Carol came the night before to help us set up the church fellowship hall for the celebration. It was almost midnight and Carol and I were still working at church. By this time, I had had a long day and was getting a headache. I didn't want to say too much to Carol about it, but she asked how I was doing. I told her I had a headache and she said, "Take an aspirin." I told her I didn't want to. She said it again, "Why don't you just take an aspirin?" Again I said more emphatically, "No, I don't want to!" She looked at me and said, "You're pregnant!" I almost cried, but didn't. I was only a couple of months along and not showing yet, but I was very tired. I never wanted to take any kind of drugs when I was pregnant. I asked her not to say anything to anyone as I wanted to tell Dad and Mom after their party the next day. I didn't want to intrude on their special day. The celebration indeed went well and many of Dad and Mom's friends and coworkers from Red Wing came to the reception.

During this same time, we had been thinking about moving because of our expanding family. We had purchased a lot in a brand-new area in Plymouth just across Hwy 169, only a couple of miles away from our home in New Hope. We designed the house ourselves this time—a three-bedroom walkout rambler with attached garage and an unfinished basement. It was in a cul de sac on a high point of the property with a south facing walkout to the back yard. We were the first ones to buy a lot in the cul de sac but the second ones to move in. The house on the lot right next to ours was built and the family moved in before our house was finished. Our new neighbors were the Bob and Maureen Myers family. Maureen and I became fast friends, and I would stop in to see her every time I went to check on our house. She had recently had a baby boy, Ted, in November 1977. They also had an older boy, Todd, who was two years older than Brian, and a girl, Beth, who was one year older than Tina.

Meanwhile, we sold our house on Gettysburg Ave in New Hope on September 1, 1978 and rented a two-bedroom apartment for the next six months until our home was finished. The apartment was in the Burgundy Apartment Complex in New Hope, just south of our Gettysburg house. One of the bedrooms was quite small and just fit our queen-size bed. The second bedroom was very large and fit the kids' twin beds easily with lots of room to spare for us to set up a crib when our new baby arrived. The baby was due within the six months we had rented the apartment. We also had a rollaway bed we could set up in that room when needed. In the single car garage that came with the apartment, we stored the rest of our furniture, yard equipment, and belongings that we couldn't get into the apartment so that we didn't have to rent any other place for storage. We ended up living there the full six months until our new house was finished.

To complicate those next six months, Brian was starting first grade. He would be going to our grade school at Grace Lutheran Church in Fridley, fifteen miles away. Tina was starting kindergarten and we put her in the Zachary Lane Elementary School which was the one closest to where our new house would be. At that time our church school did not have kindergarten.

Now at six months pregnant, I would get everyone up early enough to eat breakfast, pack a lunch for Brian, and take them out to Fridley to drop Brian off at school, go back to drop Tina off at kindergarten, go check out the house that was being built, pick Tina up at noon from school, go to the apartment to eat lunch, and go back out to Fridley to pick up Brian when he was done at school. Then we'd go back to check out the house one more time before going home.

Also during that fall, my parents came to stay with us in the apartment on and off for a few weeks since their house wasn't finished in

Detroit Lakes, and it was too cold for them to stay in the cabin. We set up the rollaway bed for them when they came. By November their house was finished, but they came down again when I was due to have our new baby. They helped get the kids to and from school. The apartment was crowded, but peaceful; and they were there to help with the children while I was in the hospital. Thank You, Lord, for how You work things out for our good!

> *And we know that all things work together for good*
> *to them that love God, to them who are*
> *the called according to his purpose.*
> *Romans 8:28*

At last, it was time for our new child to be born. Because this child was a butt first breach delivery, according to the ultrasound, I had an appointment set up to go into the hospital to be induced. Although the delivery was much more difficult than any of the others, we were excited to have another child coming.

On Saturday, November 11, 1978, Jeffrey Allen Radichel was born. I liked to say, "He came in on a 747!" since he was born at 7:47 p.m. I know they got that right because I was watching the clock. He did not cry at all when they quickly put him up on the counter in front of me and began to clean him up. Phil was with me the entire time as he had been with Brian and Tina. My head was pounding from the intense amount of pushing I was required to do to get this child born.

As a medically trained person, I was watching the clock. I knew that brain damage could occur if the child did not breathe within the first three minutes. He was not crying as most children do immediately upon birth. I said to Phil, "Why don't you baptize that child?" He ignored me as he was intent on watching everything they were doing for him. One minute had passed and the second hand was still moving quickly. I said again, "Phil, why don't you baptize that child?"

I knew the importance of baptizing from my confirmation days. Still no response from Phil or crying from the baby! Finally, the second hand was into the third minute, and I belted out one more time, "Phil, would you baptize that baby!!!" Phil turned around and looked at me and just motioned to me with his hand as he quietly said, "He's fine." With that said, I exclaimed, "Then someone give me something for my head, it's pounding!" At last, a nurse gave me some medicine to calm me down and relieve my severe headache. Thank You, Lord, for helping me through this difficult delivery and giving us a healthy baby boy!

Jeff weighed in at 8 lbs. 0.5 oz. and was 21" long. His head measured 14" around and his chest was 13.5". Imagine that head with his feet on each side of it and you know why the birth was traumatic. At this time and by our Lord's grace, our congregation had a brand-new minister, Pastor Daniel Fleischer. He came and baptized Jeffrey into the Christian faith on Sunday, November 12. Again, Uncle Ed and Auntie Verona Lentz were the godparents. Thank You, Lord, for Your blessing upon this baptism and the joy we have in receiving this gift from You. We pray Jeffrey continues to live in Your name and by Your grace.

We finally moved into our new home at 11735 50th Place, Plymouth, in February 1979. What a joy it was to have three bedrooms again. We had a master bedroom that easily fit our king-size bed and dresser. We made a walk-through bathroom on the main floor that was both a private bathroom for our bedroom when you locked the main door, and the bathroom for the main floor. Brian and Tina each had their own bedroom. We had Jeff's crib set up in Tina's bedroom for a while until Jeff was old enough to sleep in a twin bed. At that point we bought Tina a new bedroom set and bunked the two twin beds in Brian's room until we finished the lower level.

Since I had turned from sewing to cake decorating, we designed a kitchen counter that was 4' x 16' and included the sink so I could build and decorate cakes of all kinds and sizes on that counter. Many nights—late into the night or all night—I would make cakes for our children's birthdays or friends' anniversaries or weddings. I so enjoyed doing it.

Meanwhile, the door table from our last house was turned into another desk—this time for computers. It is still in Phil's shop and holds several of his servers and/or computers he uses for his church work. It is indeed an old door and has given us a huge return on our investment of time and money. We have continued to live in this home for more than forty-two years.

Three years after Jeff was born, the Lord fulfilled our early marriage desires and gave us our fourth child, another boy, to complete what we had asked for back in our dating years and early marriage. We knew the Lord had a purpose for him as well, though at the time we weren't aware of it. We did know that He wanted us to bring him up *"in the nurture and admonition of the Lord"* (Ephesians 6:4).

And so, on Saturday, December 5, 1981, at 2:31 p.m., Neal Andrew Radichel was born. Although this baby had been in the breech position for eight months, he turned during the last month for a normal delivery. It's a good thing for me he did turn because he weighed 9 lbs. 8 oz. and was 22" long. His head measured 14.25" around and his chest was 13.5". Because of his size, they still had to deliver his shoulders at an angle, one at a time. They had considered whether they would need to do a C-section, but when he turned, it wasn't necessary. Thank You, dear Father, for taking care of me again and giving us a healthy baby.

On the following Wednesday, December 9, at the evening Lenten service, Pastor Daniel Fleischer baptized Neal. According to Pastor Fleischer, it was the first time he had ever baptized a baby at an evening service. Taking Neal home from the hospital without being baptized was very traumatic for me. I was concerned that we could have an accident or something else could happen before his baptism. *"Oh ye of little faith*" (Matthew: 6:30), I should have remembered Who was in charge. Thank You, dear Lord, for these four blessings You have given us. May they grow in faith and in Your grace as they

Serve the LORD with gladness.
Psalm 100:2

Our four children now spanned ten years in age. Brian turned ten years old seven weeks after Neal was born. Brian and Tina were one year apart in school. There were six school years between Tina and Jeff, while only three years between Jeff and Neal; and still they got along pretty well over their growing up years as they each grew in the fear and the knowledge of their Lord and Savior. They followed each other in the types of activities they did and continued to take care of each other as they matured into adulthood.

Of course, there were the usual human childhood disagreements and arguments, but they were all disciplined in much the same way, and scripture would often be quoted during these times. As parents, we lived by Ephesians 6:4, "*And, ye fathers, provoke not your children to wrath: but bring them up in the nurture and admonition of the Lord.*" At the same time, the Lord says in Proverbs 13:24, "*He that spareth his rod hateth his son: but he that loveth him chasteneth him betimes.*" Or as I would say it quickly, "Spare the rod and spoil the child." They knew what that meant!

My personal thoughts on discipline reflected how I was disciplined as a child. These thoughts grew as I observed other parents disciplining, or not disciplining, their children plus what I had learned through the scriptures throughout my life. Basically, I feel it's the first five years of a child's life that have the biggest impact on how they treat others. Discipline should be immediate and fit the situation and the child. Then the next five years it's the honing and toning of the way each child acts and treats others and relates the discipline to how the Lord thinks of what was done and to whom. Then, in our case, we both strongly felt they were ready to go off to our Christian high school (Immanuel Lutheran High School) in Eau Claire, Wisconsin, a hundred miles away where they would be in a position and mindset to discipline themselves in their day-to-day relationships in a Christian setting with all of their teachers and house parents being of the same faith. We were only a phone call away if either the child or an adult had any issue to discuss.

Some of the specific incidents that I think of with our children and our specific discipline for each may sound humorous or heavy, depending on an individual's personal thoughts on the subject. But every child is different in what they need and how discipline is given. One thing was sure, they were to be quiet in church, even as young children. If they couldn't sit still, they would be taken out, either talked to or spanked depending on their age and the circumstances that morning. We didn't sit in the back of the church because most people with little children sat back there where they could watch all the other children and thus learn bad habits and not pay attention to the service. We chose to sit in the front or second pew of the church where our children could see what was going on during the service and pay attention. I learned this from my mother when I was a child!

Our firstborn, Brian, grew fast and big. He walked early and talked early. He even began to read by the time he was eighteen months. He loved to try to do things, right or wrong, but I could look at him sternly and say, "No." If he didn't stop it, I could give him a swift, firm swat on his bottom with my hand, even with a diaper on, and he would stop what he was doing. As he got a year or two older, my hand wasn't strong enough, so I started using a ruler to swat his bottom once, or twice if he needed it. By the time he was in school, neither my hand nor a ruler was enough to get his attention, so I used an old shade stick that I kept in a kitchen drawer. One firm swat with that would take care of whatever the situation was. The noise of the crack of the stick was more emphatic than the actual feel of the stick. It wasn't long after that, if he didn't stop whatever it was I didn't like, all I had to do was rattle the kitchen drawer and he would stop what he was doing. Then we would have a little talk with some added scripture to emphasize the principle of his error. He would say he was sorry, and I would forgive him.

The discipline time I enjoyed the most with Brian was when he was in his early 20s. He had been away from home for several years, both during his high school days and at college. He was smarting off to me, in a fun way as an adult. He kept it up for a while even though I said, "Enough already." So, I told him to put both hands on the kitchen counter. He questioned me and I said, "Just do it." He laughed and said, "You're kidding, right?" I went to the kitchen drawer, opened it, and took out the shade stick and said, "I don't care how old you are, you won't smart off to your mother," and then gave him a swat on his bottom. He just hooted and we had a great laugh over it. He gave me a hug, and we enjoyed the time together. He hasn't done that again, at least not that I remember.

Tina was all girl. If I didn't like something she was doing, I would scold her and she would start to cry. Then I would take some time to explain to her why what she was doing was wrong. If she persisted in it, then I would give her a swat with my hand. She needed very little discipline and was more help than not. She did like to tattle on the boys, but then that was also the female side of her as she knew what I expected of each of them. She got her share of spankings, but not nearly what Brian had received.

There was one time though when I caught Tina in the hall after she had done something I didn't like and was running away. I was mad at her and chewing her out verbally with my finger pointed at her. She just looked at me and smiled from ear to ear. I stopped right in the middle of what I was saying and took her by the hand and sat down on a chair with her in front of me, eye to eye. She didn't know what to think and was obviously nervous about what I was going to do. I asked her in a calm voice, "What were you thinking when I was reprimanding you?" She said, "What?" So I repeated the question and told her I just wanted to know. She said without a pause, "I thought you looked so funny when you were yelling at me." I just laughed and told her the story of when my mother had stopped me in the hall after I had done something she didn't like and how funny I thought she looked. Then I thanked Tina for being honest with me and sent her back to play. Life sometimes comes back to haunt you!

About that same time, my mother caught Tina in our bedroom looking at herself in our full-length mirror and imitating me by pointing her finger at the image in the mirror and saying, "Now don't you do that!" Then she would just giggle at how she looked and do it again. My mother came out to the kitchen where I was and told me all about it, enjoying the moment that she saw her granddaughter mimicking her mother (me). My thought was, "The acorn doesn't fall far from the tree—for either one of us."

What I remember most about Jeff's discipline is the very first time I reprimanded him. He was a nursing baby, but at two weeks old the doctor wanted me to begin to give him some spoon-fed cereal. He did well for a couple of days and then one day I put a small bite in his mouth, and he spit it back at me. I took my two fingers and gently, but with firmness, tapped his lips. His head twitched with the tap. He didn't even cry, but he never spit his food out again! That's about all I remember about disciplining Jeff. I'm sure he had his moments, but it fit right in with the other house discipline that was going on.

We had great neighbors and our kids played together a lot. Tina and Beth developed a strong bond over the years and since they were the only girl in each of the families, they became as close as sisters. The boys did lots of outdoor things together but were boys in actions to one another as well. At one point I was working in my office and looked out the front window where two of the boys seemed to be wrestling with each other. It looked like an older boy was hassling Jeff. The other boys were standing around as if cheering their own sibling on, almost encouraging them to get tougher on the other one. I was trying to see if they would take care of their disagreements themselves. Finally, the big boys said it was time to stop and pulled them apart. I have no idea what the squabble was about, but it was enlightening to see how they all quelled the argument themselves. Thank You, Lord.

> *Avenge not yourselves, but rather give place unto wrath: for it is written, Vengeance is mine; I will repay, saith the LORD.*
> Romans 12:19

I don't remember much discipline needed for Neal. Neal was born big and grew bigger and very strong. The best thing I think of about learning discipline when I think of Neal, happened after he was first married and they were living in their own house in a different city. Several people were out by the pool that came with this house. Brian was there, we were there, and I believe more people were there, but I don't remember who. Brian was giving Neal a hard time about something and hassling him. Finally, Neal had enough and literally picked up his bigger brother, Brian, and threw him in the pool, clothes and all. We all gasped, and Brian came to the surface laughing. He said, "I can't believe you did that!" Neal just said, "That'll teach you to talk to me that way." I didn't hear the conversation, but Neal obviously didn't like it. Oh, the fun of watching discipline from those who understand the need, at any age.

Jeff and Neal got along well as siblings. Jeff would often watch out for his little brother whenever they were together. In some of our family pictures you can see Jeff with his caring hand on Neal. When

Jeff turned twenty-one, he had some buddies take him out for his first drink at a bar. He had one too many to drink and was not feeling well when he got home, so he walked around the back yard for a while until he could come in and go to bed. He wasn't about to have his younger brother have that problem when he turned twenty-one, so Jeff took Neal out for his first drink so he wouldn't have that same experience as Jeff did. All went well. Thank you, Jeff, for being a true friend to your younger brother.

One of the early childhood activities we did with our children was to introduce them to music. It started from the day they were born as I would sing to them many times during the day, but especially as they were put to bed at night. Whether it was me putting them to bed or their father, they always were sung to after they said their prayers. We often had music playing on the stereo during the day if they were home and not in school.

When we lived in the Oregon Estates apartment in New Hope, my Aunt Janey was moving out of Minneapolis and wanted to get rid of her piano. She gave it to me just for coming to her condo and picking it up. She was moving to the Seattle, Washington, area and didn't want to haul it out there. What a blessing that piano has been to us, our children, and even our grandchildren ever since.

When Brian was less than one year old, he would walk over to the piano and gently hit the keys with his fingers to make music. Later, I would put him on my lap and play some simple tunes, mostly hymns or Bible songs, and sing to him. He loved it! Before he was three years old, I had heard of a new music school for preschoolers and older called Yamaha Music School. I enrolled Brian. His teacher, who had started the school, was Mrs. Deanna Carlson. When I told her what Brian was doing on the piano, she was excited to have him start. I was always there with him as he learned by hearing and playing with simple fingering on the keyboard. He loved it, and so did I!

The joy of having music in the house daily filled the house with energy and excitement. Each one of our children benefited from hearing, singing, and playing music as they each started Yamaha Music School at the age of three. By the time Brian was in fourth grade, he had completed the Yamaha Music training and began private lessons with Mrs. Luana Mitchell, who had been one of his Yamaha teachers and who was excited to have Brian as a private student. Luana eventually taught all four of our children the basics of music and beyond. We have enjoyed the outstanding tutoring by Luana over the years. I even enjoyed taking voice lessons from Luana which kept my voice in good working order beyond what it might have been otherwise. I enjoyed doing personal concerts for the residents in the seniors' building my mother lived in after my father passed away and sang at many weddings and funerals for our church. It was a blessing for me to bring musical joy and comfort to so many people.

As our children got into grade school, we also added summer lessons for them on different musical instruments from the Schmidt Music Store including trumpet, flute, drums, saxophone, and violin. They all took the Minnesota Music Teachers' Association (MMTA) exams, many of which they passed "With Excellence." They even wrote their own music and played them in MMTA recitals. What a joy to hear them grow in music!

Tina also started taking dance lessons before she went to kindergarten through Kay Marie and Carol's School of Dance and later with The Dance Shoppe. She took ballet (which later included toe), jazz, and tap lessons, and was in the Minnesota Dance Contest many different times both as a solo dancer and in the dance lines, winning many awards over the years. She loved doing it all but stopped dancing before starting her eighth-grade year to focus on her confirmation classes and prepping for her high school years. She continued with piano lessons through ninth grade.

As our children came along and were growing up, we took many vacations during the summers and during some of their school breaks. One of the places we enjoyed visiting was Disney World. When Epcot opened in October 1982, we took Brian and Tina only. Brian was ten and Tina was nine. They were just the right age for this new park within the Disney complex. The kids had a great time except for one attraction called the Circle Vision Theater. It was a 360-degree picture and no matter where you stood, the film was showing all around you. Brian got dizzy. Fortunately, there were handrails in rows so when you walked in, everyone just followed the rows and could use the handrail on either side of you depending where you were looking on the circle screen. The rails didn't help him though, even when Phil told him to close his eyes. But both kids loved the rest of the park.

In 1985, we took just Jeff and Neal this time to Disney World. Jeff was seven years old, and Neal was four. We stayed on the grounds of the park itself so we could walk anywhere we wanted. The boys enjoyed everything, and we enjoyed being able to party with just the two of them.

Then in October 1993, we took all four of the kids together to Disney World. We had just started a thirty-year vacation plan with Royal Holiday Club and could exchange our weeks with RCI International as well. The first week we used with this package was to Orlando for this special trip. By this time the kids were almost twenty-two, twenty, fifteen, and twelve. They got along well during the whole trip. Brian and Tina watched out for Jeff and Neal, and yet they still enjoyed all the same types of rides and adventures. It was a great time in Florida for all six of us.

Other places we visited during their growing up years were locations like Christmas Mountain Village in Wisconsin Dells, Breezy Point Resort in Minnesota, Three Bears by Wisconsin Dells, and trips to the Black Hills of South Dakota. One of the trips we made to the Black Hills was when Brian was away and not with us. It was just Tina, Jeff, and Neal. We rented a large van and took a tent with us as well. We could put the back seat of the van down and make a bed for Phil and me. Tina slept in the reclining middle seat, while Jeff and Neal wanted to sleep in the tent. Phil got up a couple of times during the night to check on the boys and told me there were deer roaming out there too, but they didn't come by the tent. I think he spent a lot of time checking on the boys. Once again, the kids enjoyed the trip, the adventure, and the tent.

Of course, we spent lots of time at my parents' cabin on Elbow Lake. At one point in the early 1970s my dad and mom decided they needed to add to the cabin. Our families were beginning to grow and there just wasn't enough sleeping or eating room. So, they decided to almost double the size of it by adding one big room which would serve as a living room and as an additional sleeping area. I was pregnant with Tina at the time and Carol with Jay. Brian was around a year old. Phil and my dad laid the foundation and put up the walls over a couple of weekends. Jim was there when the roof went on. The ladies watched the kids and made the meals. When it was all done, it indeed made a big difference in the amount of room. We could now put kids to bed in the bedrooms, and the adults could be in the added room without disturbing the kids.

Later the guys were going to add a concrete step to get into the front door of the new room. They formed up the step and began mixing concrete to pour in the frame. They got the step poured and while it was drying, Brian thought he would go in the cabin that way. Being a little over a year old he was very active. Suddenly I heard Phil yell, "Bri-an!!!" We all looked to see what was happening as Phil grabbed Brian by the shoulders to get his legs out of the fresh concrete. He took him down to the lake to wash him off. Then they had to go back and re-trowel and fill the hole left by Brian in the concrete. We were thankful that he hadn't fallen over in it or gotten any in his face. Thank You, Lord, for watching over our son.

While at the cabin over the years, we added other items of interest for our growing families. One year we put up a rope swing. It was a thick, heavy rope, like a barge rope. It was tied up in the fork of an overhanging branch of a large tree and hung almost down to the ground. A knot big enough to sit on was made at the bottom of the rope. You could then swing in any direction, holding your feet up, laying back, and pumping to get yourself to go higher. We called it the "monkey swing" since the kids loved to think they could swing like the monkeys do in the trees. My mother always liked to make up songs to sing to the kids, so she added a line to one of her songs about playing on the monkey swing. I would also sing it to our kids when they would go to bed at night at home. They loved going to the cabin with their grandparents. Whether it was playing cards or fishing, a great time was had by all! Tina especially loved Grandma's breakfast of homemade cracked wheat cereal. All the children learned a lot from their grandparents and respected them as well.

Likewise, ye younger, submit yourselves unto the elder.
I Peter 5:5a

The grade school years for all four children were fun years for us as parents. All four children went to public kindergarten in our local schools since our church didn't start kindergarten in its school until after Neal had already started first grade. Public kindergarten was a testing ground for each of them to see how they would react in a school setting. I would also say that each of the four kindergarten teachers had a different approach, which was appropriate since each child had different gifts and a different attitude.

Of the four different teachers they had, I especially cherish the education I received in looking at the gifts of our children from the eyes of Brian's kindergarten teacher, Mrs. Janet Parker (now McDowell). We met her at a pre-school meeting when we registered Brian. She was a cheerful, friendly teacher and obviously anxious to teach our child. She told us all the different types of things the children would be doing during the morning session which Brian was in. The eye opener came at the first parent-teacher conference we had just a few months later. Mrs. Parker's comment as soon as we sat down was, "So, when were you going to tell me?" It seems she thought his gifts were going to need different types of teachers because he wouldn't do well in an ordinary classroom. When we told her he was going to be going to our one-room grade school at our church, she was pleased. She said he would do well there in that type of setting with all the activity going on for all classes. And she was right, he did. It was eye-opening to see the blessings all our children would have in the setting of our church school training. Thank You, Lord, for the gift of Your daily Word not only in their grade school devotions but in the spiritual classroom discipline they would also receive.

Coming from a large school with more than twenty children in one class and then going into a small school with several grades in one classroom can be a challenge for most children. You now have different class levels of education going on while the other children in the same room are working on their assignments for their classes. Our children for the most part handled this quite well. The one who had some difficulty with this situation was Neal. He hadn't done as well academically as we thought he should from the good grades he had earned in the early grades. By the time he got to sixth grade he was taking some remedial work to catch up on a few subjects. He was also having some personal issues that we could never decipher, and I was even questioning whether he should go to ILC, but by the time he was halfway through the eighth grade it was very apparent that he was ready to go. And he did well after that. Thank You, Lord, prayers answered again!

The effectual fervent prayer of a righteous man availeth much.
James 5:16b

As our children went through all eight grades at Grace Lutheran School, they each had several teachers along the way. Our school started with just one teacher, Miss Carol Heisel, and grew from there. Besides Miss Heisel, our children also were blessed with these teachers during the eighteen years we had children at Grace Lutheran: Mrs. Karen Strike, Miss Phyllis Schuler, Miss Lila Schmidt, Mrs. Beth Sydow, Mr. James Lau, and Miss Mary Timm. There were many school volunteers from the congregation who came in along the way to help teach music, art, German, or other special classes that gave the children added benefits in their education. Each of these volunteers was a blessing to our school and our children.

Meanwhile, a sidelight blessing to me personally was the sixty miles per day that I drove our children out to school and back. That gave me fifteen miles each way to work on memory work with them. Since I had been blessed with a Christian grade school experience as well, I had learned Luther's *Small Catechism* along with many Bible verses and was therefore able to listen to their memory work and correct or help them as they recited and I drove. Our time in the car each way, regardless of the amount of traffic we had during rush hour or road construction, was always used as a profitable time for each of them. And would you believe that one of the great blessings I personally had was the continual review of my Bible history and catechism as well. I had a total of 178,200 miles of being alone with my children and our Lord during those eighteen years of taking them to school. What a blessing for any parent. Thank You, Lord!

During the early 1980s, when some of our children were in grade school, our congregation was in the process of building a new church building and fellowship hall on the same grounds as the current church at that time. It was going to be attached to the existing building. The plan was to build the new church and turn the old church into a full parsonage for the pastor and his family. At that time the parsonage and the church were one building. The basement was a large room with a kitchen which was used for church meetings, fellowship, and the school. I was also doing secretarial work for the pastor at that time.

A typical day for me when I took Brian and Tina to school was to sit in the kitchen part of the school room and enter communion attendance records for the pastor while listening to the lessons that were presented to the students. Or if we were working on cleaning up the area where the new building was going to be built, I would go out to help clear trees or shrubs. I would also go to local businesses to get quotes on materials we would need for different projects. Phil and I worked sort of like a general contractor for the entire project. We also worked on the church most weekends, and our children would go with us. I especially remember Jeff and Neal as babies. I would take a playpen along, and whoever the baby was at the time would play or sleep in the playpen for much of the day. The older children who were there, if not helping their parents with the work, would also keep an eye on my babies and let me know if they needed anything. It took five to seven years to get through all the building of the new church/ fellowship hall and remodeling of the parsonage.

As the major work of digging the hole for the building and setting up the pre-stressed concrete walls of the church and fellowship hall continued, I took pictures of all that was going on and along with other women of our congregation helped with serving lunches and coffee breaks for the workers. Many of the workers were from our own congregation, especially in the remodeling of the parsonage and finishing of the new church building. All this time our children were attending school. In fact, the church building structure was finally completed, and we had Christmas services in the fellowship hall in December 1985. It took a few more months of interior finishing work before we were worshipping in the new sanctuary. One of my fond memories of finishing the new church narthex was taking the cornerstone out of the old church, which was built in 1958, and adding that to the wall in the narthex next to the new cornerstone which said 1985. I loved the look of simply switching the two numbers from 58 to 85.

Brian was confirmed in the new church on May 18, 1986, by Pastor Daniel Fleischer. His was the first confirmation class in the church his parents helped build. His Bible verse, which I wrote on the cake I made for his reception, was 1 Corinthians 6:20. When I think about it, I remember that I was the first confirmation class in the church I helped my parents build in Red Wing, and my mother was the first confirmation class in the church that her father, my grandpa Otto, helped build in Sioux City, Iowa. Thank You, Lord for giving us the heritage of working in Your church and knowing the joy of serving You.

In the following years:

Tina was confirmed on May 31, 1986, by Pastor Daniel Fleischer. Her Bible verse was Psalm 37:5.

Jeff was confirmed on May 16, 1993, by Pastor Daniel Fleischer. He wrote an essay for his confirmation, as each class member did. His essay was "Why is it important not only to confess "God", but to confess the Triune God before the World?"

Neal was confirmed on May 12, 1996, by Pastor Daniel Fleischer. His Bible verse was Ephesians 2:8-9.

Lo, children are an heritage of the LORD.
Psalm 127:3a

Born and raised in light of Scripture
Seeking first the Word of God;
Then to raise those whom God gives us
Brings to mind the roads we've trod.

Looking back at our beginnings
Where He took us on our way,
Gave us insight how to parent
Those He gave us day by day.

Chapter 6

Our Children's Education and Work Lives

Yes, I have a goodly heritage.

Psalm 16:6b

After eight years in grade school at Grace Lutheran in Fridley, Minnesota, our children started ninth grade at Immanuel Lutheran High School & College (ILC), our synod's parochial school in Eau Claire, Wisconsin. It is a campus for high school, college, and seminary with dorms for students who are not living in or near Eau Claire. Some people will say, "How can you send your fourteen-year-old child a hundred miles away to live on a campus during their teenage years?" It goes back to our basic beliefs about discipline based on Proverbs 22:6, *"Train up a child in the way he should go: and when he is old, he will not depart from it."* By the time children get into high school, their patterns of life and knowing right from wrong are pretty much engrained in their personality. In fact, one of my sayings I would say to our children as I left them at school was, "If you can't be good, have fun." Then I would look them in the eye, pointing my finger heavenward, and continue with, "Just remember Who's watching!"

After a while, they would say the second part after I said the first part, so I knew they knew what I meant by it.

When they are put into a setting with the same principles of discipline based on scripture that they grew up learning, and have responsible adults as their mentors and caregivers, enrolling them in a school at a distance is easier to do. Yes, Phil and I did a lot of traveling during the school year, driving to Eau Claire for Friday night events at school and then bringing them home once a month or so for a weekend at home. Yes, we did talk to our children during the week if we, or they, had particular questions or concerns. Their friends were always fellow Christians in the faith, and they were blessed daily with a morning chapel and professors and teachers of their faith. All four of our children graduated from the high school program at ILC. Three of our four children eventually married someone from their ILC days, and one child married a wonderful Christian woman who attended a different school.

Brian started high school at ILC in the fall of 1986, or as he would say, during the days of *Top Gun*, *Hunt for Red October*, and Tom Clancy. While at ILC, Brian took Choir, singing tenor, and participated in Tour Choir as well. He was an alternate for the Tour Choir as a freshman, singing only in Eau Claire and some congregations in Minnesota. During his sophomore year he was part of the Tour Choir as they went to our congregations in Michigan. In his junior year, they went to Colorado and Wyoming where he also played trumpet with some of the music, thanks to his earlier musical training. During his senior year the Tour Choir went throughout Minnesota, and he again accompanied some of the music on his trumpet. What a joy it was for him to play and sing praises to his Lord!

After the many years Brian had taken piano in grade school, he was ready to move on to something different in high school. He said he had enough of piano. We still felt he would benefit by continuing his music training, but switching to organ. Therefore, as a freshman at ILC, he started lessons on organ with Professor Robert Dommer. He continued that for two years. As he started his junior year, he took lessons from ILC's new organ teacher, Professor John Reim. Little did any of us know that only seven years after Brian graduated from high school, he would be playing a little electric keyboard for a new congregation in Atlanta, Georgia. He has continued as a church organist from that time on. After moving to Dallas, Texas, he played a big pipe organ for his congregation there. God's hand was truly in his life.

Brian also played trumpet in the pep band and was the Pep Club president his senior year. For sports he chose baseball and basketball all four years, being the basketball manager in his sophomore through senior years. He was honored to be the master of ceremonies for the 1990 Class Day at the end of his senior school year.

During the summers of his high school days, Brian mostly worked at the Golden Valley Country Club as a caddy as well as in the rack room. He got the job through his cousin, Paul Lentz, who worked at the country club as a waiter in the dining room.

Brian became determined to make it to the U.S. Naval Academy with the hope of becoming a submarine officer. The summer before his high school senior year, in 1989, he attended Candidate Camp at the Naval Academy with the prospective class that would graduate in 1994. Later that fall, he received his nomination from Rep. Bill Frenzel of Minneapolis. Unfortunately, he failed to get an appointment due to his eyes, which hadn't been good since fourth grade when he got his glasses.

That fall of 1990, instead of going to the Naval Academy as he had wanted to do, Brian went to the University of Minnesota (U of M) and joined the Navy Reserve Officer's Training Corps (ROTC), while majoring in electrical engineering. Having done his "dorm time" at ILC, Brian moved home to our house, rather than live on campus, and commuted to downtown Minneapolis.

While at the U of M, Brian tried to cruise through school like he did at ILC. It eventually caught up to him, however, and he posted a grade point of 1.0 (out of 4.0) in the winter quarter of 1992. That got him put on academic probation from both the university and ROTC. During his spring semester he managed three A grades but still got a D in differential equations, and that, combined with his spotty tardy record (too early and too far to go from Plymouth for 6:00 a.m. ROTC formation) cost him his naval career. He was separated that summer of 1992 as a midshipman second class and the Navy dream was over. He was able to recover academically, however, and spent the summer passing his remaining sophomore courses to continue at the U of M. God had other plans for Brian.

A man's heart deviseth his way: but the LORD directeth his steps.
Proverbs 16:9

During his time at college, Brian worked first at Burger King, then Holiday Plus at the lunch counter and in the photo lab. Between the fall of 1992 and 1993 Brian worked at Byerly's food store in the coffee bar and deli. In the fall of 1993, as he started his fourth year at the U of M, Brian started working at KEBCO (now KEB America, Inc., a drive and automation systems company) on an engineering internship in motor controls and AC drives. His navy credits and academic struggles cost him a couple of quarters, however, and it took a fifth year to complete his coursework, graduating in August of 1995 with a Bachelor of Electrical Engineering degree.

Earlier, in June of 1995, though Brian had one full-time class remaining before graduation, he started full-time at KEBCO as an application engineer and IT helper. When he came home from his first day of full-time work, Phil and I took him out on the screen porch alone and popped a bottle of champagne. We welcomed Brian to the "adult members of the family" and Phil gave him an offer: Brian could continue to live at home, I would wash his clothes, and he could continue to eat with us, and come and go as he pleased—all for (as Phil put it) the "reasonable sum of $700 a month." Brian said, "But I can get an apartment near the office (now in Mendota Heights) for only $660!" Phil's response: "I'll help you move." Neal was finishing seventh grade at the time, Jeff had just come home from ILC, finishing his high school sophomore year, and Tina had just graduated (the first time) from UW-Eau Claire.

Brian moved out July 1, 1995, to a one-bedroom apartment in Eagan, just south of Minneapolis. About a month later he called his dad and said, "Wait a minute . . . between my rent, food, utilities, insurance, etc., this is costing me like $1200 a month!" Then, quoting an ancient cinematic knight, which is now famous in Brian's family, his dad said, "My son, you have chosen . . . poorly."

Trust in the LORD with all thine heart;
and lean not unto thine own understanding.
Proverbs 3:5

Tina started high school at ILC in Eau Claire in the fall of 1987 and enjoyed the many activities available in sports with volleyball, softball, and as a cheerleader. She participated in the arts with plays and musicals, which included the Tour Choir in her senior year. Between her junior and senior year, she received a brochure for the People-to-People High School Student Ambassador Program and decided she wanted to go on one of their European trips. This was the summer after the Berlin Wall came down in 1990. We were intrigued by this educational trip she was going to make and continued in prayer for her safety while she was gone. The trip lasted about a month. At least she knew one member of the thirty students on the trip. It turned out one of our church members, Steve Gunther, was also going on this trip. When I asked Tina what she thought about busing across the Berlin Wall, she said, "We weren't actually in Berlin, but we crossed West Germany to East Germany and our bus driver, who had been driving for thirty years, was shocked and said, 'Where are all the guards?' The checkpoint was empty—literally. We didn't even slow down. As soon as we crossed the border, it felt like we went from color to black and white, from middle class to poverty." This was quite an event for a seventeen-year-old student.

Tina graduated from ILC in the spring of 1991. That fall, Tina stayed in Eau Claire and enrolled at the University of Wisconsin—Eau Claire, majoring in communication sciences & disorders. She moved into the University dorms and stayed there for the next two years. She kept in touch with ILC and her friends there. Because of Tina's dance training in grade school, she offered to help with ILC's 1992 spring musical *West Side Story* where she worked with Sarah Pfeiffer, a classmate, and the play director, Wayne Eichstadt, who was in the ILC seminary at the time. She also started working with Prof. Paul D. Nolting, who was volunteering with the Hugh O'Brian Youth (HOBY) leadership program, a seminar/leadership program for high school sophomores. When Brian was a sophomore in high school, he had gone to a HOBY program. Because of this, Tina engaged him for some help with HOBY as well. She later recruited Neal as a sophomore too. They all enjoyed the experience.

The following spring of 1993, Tina also worked the ILC musical, *Meet Me in St. Louis*, again with Sarah Pfeiffer as musical director and Wayne Eichstadt as the director/producer. This was Wayne's last year at ILC as he would be graduating and would be ordained as a minister in a CLC congregation in Tacoma, Washington. The week before the musical was to be performed, Phil and I were in Eau Claire. It was late afternoon, so we stopped in to see if Tina was in the ILC gym getting ready for the play. We walked in the door at the opposite end from the gym stage. We stopped in our tracks as we looked at the stage. No one was in the entire gym except Tina and Wayne. They were sitting about two feet apart from each other on the edge of the stage, talking. Phil paused for a quick moment, turned to me, and said quietly, "Now there's a couple!" We quietly turned around and went back out into the hall so as not to disturb them until they were done talking. The play was a huge success as was the one the year before.

After two years of college dorm life, Tina moved into a house, called the Farwell House, with her friends Miriam Leean, Nanette Breunig, and Becky Woerpel. When Miriam graduated two years later, she moved to Atlanta, Georgia and became a chiropractor. Miriam and Brian were both in Atlanta at that time so they often spent time together. Nanette and Becky continued with their teaching degrees and continued to keep in touch with Tina.

During the kids' high school years, they all worked during the summers to help with some of their school expenses. Tina always tried to make about $1,000. But college was different to start with, and we took care of the first two years for her. For the next two years, Tina had some scholarship monies and worked at the Northern States Power (NSP) call center in Eau Claire to help with her housing and other expenses. In the spring of 1995, Tina graduated magna cum laude, an academic distinction for graduates with total GPAs of 3.5–3.7 on a 4.0 scale. We were very proud of her academic accomplishment. She continued for her master's degree at UW—Eau Claire for the next two years and finished with a 4.0 GPA—straight A grades.

Tina paid for her master's education totally by herself with a work-study program the first year and then with what she earned herself the second year. In the fall of 1995, after Tina completed her undergraduate degree, she started working for Thinking Publications, a publishing company run by a speech-language pathologist and her husband, Nancy and Mike McKinley. Tina mostly did warehouse work at that time, packing materials for conventions. In the summer of 1996, Tina moved again into an apartment with a friend,

Cindy Schmidt. By the spring of 1997, when Jeff was graduating from high school at ILC, Tina graduated one day later with her master's in Communication Sciences and Disorders. Tina was now doing consulting for Thinking Publications. That fall Tina also started working at Luther Hospital in Eau Claire as a speech-language pathologist. In 1998, with everything else going on with her working life, Tina and Rev. Paul D. Nolting, one of the pastors at Immanuel Lutheran Church in Mankato, Minnesota, started a Youth Conference for CLC high school students to be held during the summer. She so enjoyed helping with the setting up of this event. She also got to work again with Wayne Eichstadt, who had taken a call as the associate pastor at Immanuel by this time. He had been the director of the two plays at ILC that Tina had worked with five to six years before this time. This conference continued every other year until 2015.

To everything there is a season,
and a time for every purpose under the heaven.
Ecclesiastes 3:1

In the fall of 1993, Jeff started ILC as a freshman in high school. During high school, Jeff enjoyed all the sports that were available: cross country, basketball, baseball, and even flag football that the kids would play on the lawn. Jeff also was part of the ILC Tour Choir, singing tenor. In his junior year they traveled through Colorado to Phoenix, Arizona, singing at our congregations along the way. In his senior year, they visited many of the congregations in the Midwest. What a blessing it was as a parent to attend several of these Tour Choir concerts and watch the joy of the congregations as they experienced these young people witnessing their faith through song (cf. Psalm 95:1).

During the summers of Jeff's high school days at ILC, from 1993–1997, he worked mostly at the Golden Valley Country Club as a golf caddy like his brother, Brian. Later he worked there in the bag room, also called the rack room, and by the time he was a freshman in college, he was working on the ground crew. He enjoyed the Country Club and the people he met over the years.

In the fall of 1997, Jeff enrolled in college at the University of Wisconsin—Eau Claire in pre-engineering. He stayed in Bridgeman Hall until the end of his sophomore year, after which time he decided to come back to Minnesota. He moved back home and, in the fall of 1999, enrolled at the University of Minnesota, majoring in mechanical engineering.

Jeff was trying to decide what he wanted to do with his life, and after his first semester at the U of M, he took a semester abroad, and did that semester of college at the University of Edinburgh, in Scotland. Part way through that semester, Phil and I decided to take a trip to go see him. What a wonderful trip it was for us to see this beautiful country.

We rented a car after landing in Edinburgh so we could tour the area. At one point during our visit, we took a side trip with Jeff to the top of a mountain called Arthur's Seat, which is part of a group of hills in Edinburgh. The views were breathtaking! Jeff and Phil were talking somewhat privately so I walked away to let them talk. Phil told me later that Jeff said to him, "I am thinking that maybe I should go into the ministry." Phil responded, "Finish what you started first, and you can always do the ministry later." They had a good discussion for a while.

Jeff told me his version of this discussion years later and said that he had been wrestling for two years to understand what his calling in life was to be. He decided that he had struggled enough with the ministry question and asked the Lord to give him direction in life through his earthly father. Jeff said he was going to just ask his dad and whatever he said, Jeff would do. Jeff said as usual his dad's first answer was, "What do you think you should do?" Jeff said he told his dad, "For once in your life you're going to give me a straight answer." Then

Jeff said that Phil was taken aback by his comment but asked him how much school he had left to do. When Jeff told him two years, Phil told him, "Finish your degree, after that you can do whatever you want." Jeff said he told him "Okay," and they didn't talk about it anymore. But Jeff did say to me that he had to think about it a little, then talked to Phil again later, and it all made sense. Jeff told me much later that it "turns out the Lord has led me to that calling in a much different way than I would have expected, allowing me to focus more on the evangelist skill set in my work." Thank You, Lord, for the relationship this father and son have developed over the years.

Back at Jeff's room, Phil brought communion wafers with us and bought some wine after we got off the plane. Phil, an elder at our church at the time, gave Jeff and me communion because Jeff hadn't had communion since he left home. Then Phil handed a wafer to Jeff and told Jeff to give him communion. What a joy it was to celebrate the Lord's Supper together with Jeff in this far away country. At the end of that semester, Jeff came back home.

Jeff had become friends with several students during his six-month stay in Edinburgh. In the fall of 2001, Jeff decided to go visit one of his friends, Mike, who lived in New York but had gone to school with Jeff in Scotland. They had a great time seeing the sights in New York City. Jeff sent me a picture that he took from the top of the Twin Towers that showed the huge New York City landscape. He took it on Saturday, September 8, 2001.

Jeff at the top of the World Trade Center on September 8, 2001

The next Tuesday, my neighbor, Maureen Myers, called at 8:00 a.m. to tell me to hurry up and turn on the TV, because a plane had flown into the Twin Towers. My heart sank as I knew Jeff was in New York

City at that time and had been visiting the Towers. After watching the horrific replay of the airplanes flying into the Towers, I left for a Mary Kay director's meeting scheduled that morning.

When I got to the meeting, I mentioned that my son was in New York and had just been on the top of that Tower a couple of days earlier. I laid my cell phone on the table, and I told them I was leaving it turned on in case my son called. In the middle of the meeting, the cell phone rang. I picked it up and went into the next room. I didn't hear another word from the meeting as they waited for me to come back. It was Jeff on the phone—thank You, Lord, he was safe. I asked him where he was; he said he was in Boston. I said, "Get on a plane and come home now!" He said calmly, "Mom, do you know where those planes came from?" I didn't know. He said, "They came from Boston." I said, "Then rent a car and drive home!" He said, "There are no cars available to rent at this time. I will get there in time, but it will take a little while. I will let you know when I'm on my way home." I thanked the Lord that he was safe, asked Jeff to keep me informed, told him he and many others were in my prayers, and wished him God-speed. When I returned to the meeting, they were all very quiet and simply asked how things were. I relayed Jeff's comments. Later that week, Jeff flew home safely. To God be the glory!

In everything give thanks.
I Thessalonians 5:18

In the summer of 2002, Jeff received his bachelor's degree in Mechanical Engineering. He had been working as a Co-op Student for The Toro Company during his time at the U of M. By this time, he was ready for his own place and bought a townhouse in New Brighton, a suburb of St. Paul. He had a couple of his buddies living with him at this time, Eli Wales and Ryan Libby. In 2003, he began working for Graco Company as a manufacturing engineer. In 2005, Jeff decided to go for his Master's in Business Administration and in 2008 got his MBA from Carlson School of Business. He then became a global product marketing manager for Graco and continued to work there until 2010. From that time on, Jeff has worked for four different companies during which time he also started his own company, The Next Step Inc., of which he is the president and owner.

One of the things Jeff did with his evangelist gift during his early working years was to use that skill in a daily devotion called, "Thought of the Day." Each morning he would email it to me, along with many others who had requested it among his family, friends, and coworkers. Each "Thought" began with a Bible verse and then comments from Jeff depending on what was going on in his life at the time. The messages reflected both his biblical background as well as his reactions to things that happened or were happening to him at the time. After many years of reading these "Thoughts" daily, I printed and kept the one he wrote on Friday, February 17, 2017. It reminded me again of the struggle Jeff had in deciding what to do with his life. Here is what he wrote:

Romans 8:35, 37 (NASB)

Who will separate us from the love of Christ? Will tribulation, or distress, or persecution, or famine, or nakedness, or peril, or sword? But in all these things we overwhelmingly conquer through Him who loved us.

Yesterday I was able to speak to a group of high schoolers at my old high school. We were talking about careers and the school had brought in several people to tell them about what they do. It reminded me of when I was in their place. How much I struggled thinking or deciding what I was going to do in life. For me in those years there were serious times of distress and frustration.

However, with more years to reflect on it, the Lord led me through those years in a way that I know was divinely guided. That throughout the journey He was working things out for my good. Through Christ we are more than conquerors. So today, let us take a moment to think back to the trials or difficulties and meditate on the ways the Lord brought us through them. To be thankful for His love and grace.

Blessings on your day . . .

I have thanked the Lord many times over for the direction in life He has given to Jeff, who has taken what he has learned from his Lord and passed it on to others. Jeff was also instrumental in his adult life in helping to start a new congregation called Living Savior Lutheran Church in the southwest part of Minneapolis where he and other CLC members were living at the time. That work, blessed by the Lord, gave Twin Cities area members three congregations to choose from, depending on where they lived. It is a joy for me, as a mother, to watch Jeff reach out to others continually not only to strengthen his own faith, but to encourage others to strengthen their own faith and gather with fellow Christians in the Word. To God be the glory!

And whatsoever ye do, do it heartily, as to the LORD,
and not unto men.
Colossians 3:23

Neal entered ILC as a freshman in high school in the fall of 1996. He was so ready to be there. Jeff was a senior when Neal started. Phil and I were now alone in the house—but not for long. Neal said he didn't know what he wanted to do when he got out of high school. At one point he thought he wanted to be a Marine or be in the Air Force or something in the military. However, he decided to stay at ILC during his freshman year in college and was encouraged to enroll in the pre-theology program. Then somewhere along the way of his college education Neal said that the Lord just had him keep going on to be a pastor, and he never turned back.

In high school Neal played basketball and baseball for all four years and did one year of cross country. He liked to play flag football on campus and did that for the eleven years he was at ILC. Neal was also in the ILC Tour Choir in college and seminary from 2000–2006.

While Neal was at ILC in high school, he mostly worked during the summers at the Golden Valley Country Club as a caddy and at Bester Bros Moving & Storage Company as a laborer for his cousin Paul Lentz. During his college and seminary days at ILC, from 2000–2007 when he graduated, he worked during the school year at the Menards Distribution Center in Eau Claire.

Neal took up game hunting during his senior year in high school. He did a lot of his hunting with Aaron Thompson, his best friend from ILC, who eventually became Neal's brother-in-love since they each married one of the daughters of Dennis and Chris Oster. They would hunt turkeys or deer in the woods around Eau Claire. Phil bought Neal a gun, a Marlin .22 gauge, which shocked me. As a medical technologist and having drawn blood on ER patients, including those with gunshot wounds, I never liked the thought of having a gun in the house. However, Neal was required to take gun safety classes and passed those. He was very careful about how he used and stored the gun. I tried to lighten up and to remember God was in charge whenever I knew Neal was going hunting. He did well and even gave us some of the meat from the animals he hunted, and it was good. He still has his gun and has even gone hunting with his brothers, his dad, and other relatives over the years. Thank You, Lord, for protecting all of them while hunting.

Neal graduated from high school at ILC in the year 2000, yes, the turn of the century. I had asked him if he wanted a class ring to commemorate that great year. He said "No." It happened that at that same time I was becoming a Mary Kay director in my Mary Kay life and the gift I got from the company was a beautiful amethyst ring. Amethyst happens to be my birth stone, and I love it. So, my comment regarding this time of Neal's graduation was always, "Neal graduated, but I got the ring!"

The summer after Neal graduated from high school, he was part of a Wisconsin team that went to Australia to play basketball. What an honor that was, and he had a great trip. The team did some fundraising, but each team member mostly paid his own way. We helped Neal fund this outstanding trip opportunity for him. They were gone ten days, having flown non-stop on the way down and then stopping in Hawaii for two days on the way back. He played eight games while there, and they won a couple of them. One of his friends, Nathan Quade, was also on this trip. Certainly, a memorable trip for an eighteen-year-old.

After high school Neal stayed at ILC through his four years of college and three years of seminary, during which time Phil said he never once heard Neal question whether he should become a minister. In his senior year in high school, Neal started dating Erin Oster, an ILC classmate. Erin's family lived in Eau Claire, so she was there year-round. During seminary the Sem students have a pastoral internship, and they are called *vicars*. They go to a host congregation within the synod to work with the host pastor, learning and performing many of the pastoral duties under the pastor's guidance. This gives them up close and personal guidance and experience on being a pastor. Neal did his internships in Fond du Lac, Wisconsin at Luther Memorial Church under Rev. David Naumann in 2005 and in Eau Claire at Messiah Lutheran Church under Rev. Paul M. Tiefel, Jr. in 2006. By this time Neal had married Erin, and they had their first child, so it was nice to be staying in Eau Claire for that second internship.

While Neal was in his last year in seminary, he and I tried to find him a gown for his ministry. We looked at the Bible stores at different gowns but couldn't really decide on any one gown. Then a true blessing came when Pastor Paul F. Nolting, father of Pastor Paul D. Nolting, gave Neal his own gown for Neal's use. Pastor Paul F. Nolting was married to Erin's grandmother, Betty. He was no longer preaching, or even guest preaching, and they were downsizing in their retirement. I was so excited to have him do that for Neal. In my mind I pictured Elijah being taken up in a fiery chariot to heaven and dropping his gown back down to Elisha to carry on the work God had for him to do (2 Kings 2:13). I so admired Pastor Paul F. Nolting for all his work over the years in our church body.

After graduation from seminary in 2007, Neal was ordained as a pastor at St. Stephen Lutheran Church and School in Mountain View, California where he began his ministry. During the ordination service, Pastor Rollin Reim, also a very special man whom God gave the church, presented Neal with a cross on a chain for him to wear around his neck on his gown. It was one that Pastor Reim had received for his ordination and wanted Neal to have it as a passing of the mantle—another true blessing for Neal as he entered the ministry.

Neal served St. Stephen congregation in Mountain View from 2007 until 2011 when he accepted a call to Luther Memorial Church and School in Fond du Lac, where he had been a vicar during his seminary years. He served Luther Memorial congregation until 2018 when he accepted a call to be an associate pastor of Immanuel Lutheran Church and School in Mankato, where he is currently serving.

While at Luther Memorial Church, Neal was instrumental in starting a men's retreat called *Man Up!* within our synod. As their website indicates, each fall they meet to "offer strength and encouragement for men 18 and older for their personal faith, family, and fellowship at church. The weekend will include Bible study, fellowship, leadership training, team building, relationship building, worship, and many outdoor bonding activities." It is a joy for me, as a mother, to watch

Neal use his ministerial talents along with his love of nature to bring others together in Christ. To God be the glory!

Phil has commented over the years that Jeff struggled in college, as did Brian. Both seemed to question what they should do. To some extent Phil thought it reflected on their post college work life where, in his viewpoint, they also seemed to struggle. Maybe Phil thought this because they both asked him for advice, whereas he didn't think Tina would have even asked since she probably didn't think she needed it. At the same time, Neal never questioned what he felt he was to do with his life. Neal, if he needed advice during his school years, didn't ask us, but deferred to his professional mentors. I do know that all our children prayed to their Lord continually throughout their college days for strength to persevere. And they all did. To God be the glory and praise!

To every thing there is a season,
and a time to every purpose under the heaven.
Ecclesiastes 3:1

As we watched each child develop
Practicing what they had learned,
Using all their God-giv'n talents,
Leaving no stone still unturned,

Many prayers we uttered daily
For their safety and their needs,
Asking God to give direction
To their issues and their needs.

Chapter 7

Our Children Mature

Therefore shall a man leave his father and his mother, and shall cleave unto his wife: and they shall be one flesh.

Genesis 2:24

In 1993, while in college, Brian started dating Sarah Marohn. He met Sarah while working at Byerly's Ridgedale in Minnetonka, a suburb of Minneapolis. Then in the fall of 1995, Brian and Sarah became engaged and were planning a wedding when Sarah graduated from Gustavus Adolphus College in St. Peter, Minnesota. However, the Lord had other plans for Brian, and in the spring of 1996, Brian and Sarah broke up. Later that summer, Brian started traveling to Atlanta for work and ultimately decided to move to Georgia to become KEBCO's (see Chapter 6) first remote direct employee.

In March of 1997, Brian packed up the apartment and took a U-Haul to Atlanta, setting up his office northwest of downtown Atlanta in Smyrna. He knew no one in Atlanta except Tina's college roommate Miriam Leean, who had moved there after she graduated from UW—Eau Claire.

Brian started dating online and met a few girls from Charlotte,

North Carolina. Since his work territory included the entire Southeast, he met with a couple of these girls at times while he was on business trips. In July of 1997, he was heading to Orlando, Florida for another business trip and remembered that a friend of one of these girls, whom he'd also talked to online, was working at Disney World. Brian arranged to meet her for dinner one night while he was there, and that turned into three or four late nights in a row talking—and a weekend spent at Disney on her guest pass. Her name was Leigh Bennett, and Brian came back to Atlanta having found a new girlfriend. In Atlanta, he continued to travel, seeing Leigh whenever he could in Charlotte, where she was a student at UNC-Charlotte. Soon Leigh started to visit Brian as much as Brian went to see her, and they were spending time together most weekends.

Our Lord continued to watch over Brian. A CLC preaching station had been meeting in Atlanta for about fourteen years—first under Rev. John Schierenbeck, then Rev. Warren Fanning—both coming from Holy Trinity congregation in West Columbia, South Carolina to serve this small group of Christians. In the fall of 1997, Brian started attending their once-a-month services in a rented hotel meeting room—which was quite small for someone who had grown up in three of the larger congregations in the CLC (Grace, Fridley; Messiah, Eau Claire; and Berea, Inver Grove Heights). Pastor Fanning left in the fall of 1997 for Phoenix, Arizona and during the vacancy, Rev. Jay Hartmann started coming up from Live Oak, Florida. In January of 1998, Pastor Hartmann asked the congregation, who recently had three new families join, "Why aren't you organized as a congregation?" According to Brian, the families looked at each other and realized that they should. Zion Evangelical Lutheran Church was born in January of 1998 with approximately thirty members and nine voters. Pastor Hartmann only came twice more, and Pastor Vance Fossum started serving the congregation from Columbia, South Carolina. Brian was elected as the first president of the congregation. The congregation began holding weekly services with the aid of an electronic keyboard. With Brian's piano and other musical training, he and Markie Everhart were the first organists of Zion. Thank You, Lord, for preparing Brian for this work in Your earthly kingdom.

Brian and Leigh continued to date and in March of 1998, Brian proposed to Leigh. He had purchased a ring for her earlier in the day, and it was burning a hole in his pocket. He picked up Leigh and took her to the A&P grocery store since he wanted to get her a card and some flowers. He asked her to wait in the car as he was only going to be a minute. When he came out, he opened the car door and handed her the flowers and card. She was so excited about the flowers and began reading the card that she hadn't noticed Brian getting down on one knee. When she looked up, he was holding the ring and asked her to marry him. He is a romantic—like his mother!

They were married on Saturday, January 9, 1999, two weeks after Leigh's graduation from UNC-Charlotte, in Leigh's home church in Randleman, North Carolina, in a beautiful service. What a joy it was for us to be with Leigh's family and really get acquainted with them. We had more time now to spend with her parents, Kay and Dickie Bennett, her brother Matt, and her grandma Vera Moser.

The wedding address was done in the New King James Version and based on I Corinthians 13, a chapter all about love (charity) ending with verse 13:

> *And now abide faith, hope, love, these three;*
> *but the greatest of these is love.*

Also from our family—Jeff was a groomsman, Tina was a bridesmaid, and Neal was an usher. Jay Sandeen, Brian's cousin, was also an usher while Phil's brother, Frank, was the videographer. Thank You, Lord, for the gift of this *daughter-in-love* to our family.

Brian and Leigh
on their Wedding Day (1999)

Since the church had a small basement and alcohol was not allowed, they had reserved a reception area in a local bowling alley. Everyone went there and enjoyed themselves at the reception. They also did a lot of bowling. Even though all were still in their wedding garments, they still bowled. Yes, even Leigh bowled in her wedding dress!

A month later, Brian and Leigh went on their honeymoon to the Nassau Marriott Resort in the Bahamas, compliments of Phil and me. What a blessing it was for us to be able to give them this special time together.

By the time of their wedding, Brian had moved up to Lake Lanier, north of Atlanta, and had an apartment overlooking the lake. Leigh joined him and Brian worked from home, still traveling around the Southeast for KEBCO. But a year later, the opportunity he was hoping for became open, and he joined Bearings & Drives Industrial in January of 2000 as an electrical engineer, helping the distributor he had called on before while working for KEBCO. He went to work for Bobby Faulkner, his engineering mentor in Georgia.

Shortly afterward, Leigh and Brian found a house in Norcross, Georgia and moved into their first home, with a swimming pool and a fenced-in lot. In the first year after they were married, we went there to help them with some house repairs—fixing broken plumbing (and the resulting water damage), a leaky roof (and the resulting water damage), and a split pool liner (which fortunately didn't cause any interior water damage). Regardless of the work that was going on at their home, we were happy to be able to go see them and help. We were experienced construction workers by this time.

Growing up with music in our home added to the joy of singing to the Lord at home, in church, and in school for all our children. On Christmas 2002, with three of our four children at home, we were opening our gifts when Jeff called Brian in Atlanta and put him on speaker. Jeff handed me a package to open. It was a CD titled "Nestled in the Quiet Beauty by The Radichel Kids." I opened the cover of the CD case and took out the folder insert. There were six pages of pictures and notes from each of the children and what part they each sang and played for the CD. They each told us how they appreciated all they were taught growing up, especially about the love of their Lord, and how they were thankful for the parents their Lord gave them. On the CD were eleven songs, each separated by a Bible verse that they had learned growing up. As they played it for us, my eyes were filled with tears.

It seems that Tina, Jeff, and Neal went to Atlanta over Thanksgiving, where Brian and Leigh were living, to record this CD. It took them the whole weekend to record the individual parts of the CD. In some of the music, Tina recorded both the soprano and the alto voices for the lady's part. In some of the music Brian played the electric piano, which could be made to sound like an organ. He also played the trumpet in some of the songs. All parts were recorded separately. Leigh spent the weekend feeding them and tending to their needs between sessions. When they got back home, Jeff would wait until Phil and I were out of the house and then start to splice it all together. There were many parts to each song. It was an engineering marvel for this college graduate, but he did it well! What a heartwarming project they made. Thank You, Lord, for these precious gifts You have given us in our children. To God be the glory!

Honor thy father and thy mother: that thy days may be long
upon the land which the LORD thy God giveth thee.
Exodus 20:12

Tina continued to work at Thinking Publications until the end of 2001 and helped them start their software development division. While still in Eau Claire as an undergraduate, Tina had become a member of WSHA (Wisconsin Speech and Hearing Association) and was elected president in 2001. She continued as president from 2002–2004 and one more year as past president in 2005. Meetings continued to take her all over Wisconsin even after she moved back to Minnesota in February 2002 and began working at AGS Publishing out of Shoreview and Circle Pines, Minnesota. That same month, on Super Bowl Sunday, February 3, 2002, Tina began dating Pastor Wayne Eichstadt. With the work Tina had been doing with the Youth Conference and taking trips to Mankato for it, she and Wayne had spent more time together. In April 2003, after they attended the Mankato State University (MSU) Theater's Saturday night production of the musical "Guys and Dolls" together, Wayne proposed to Tina. Tina continued to work at AGS while they were distance dating from Plymouth to Mankato, as she was still living with us. She did her wedding planning from home.

As I mentioned earlier, Neal, our youngest son, had started to date Erin Oster in January of his senior year in high school before graduating in 2000. They dated for a couple of years in college. Then Phil and I had a New Year's Eve party at our house on December 31, 2002, with several of our church friends. Neal and Erin were both there. As the party was drawing to a close, Neal and Erin had gone downstairs to the family room. While we were upstairs saying goodbye to the last of the guests, Larry and Susan Nelson, Neal and Erin came up the steps. It was after midnight, and they told us they were now engaged! WOW! What a way to start a New Year!

You can imagine the joy and planning that took place that year, especially after Wayne and Tina were engaged just four months later. After working around all the schedules for both couples, it ended up that Neal and Erin were going to be married that fall, the week after Wayne and Tina. What fun we had organizing showers, groom's dinners, and of course wedding invitations and receptions. It was a very busy year.

On Saturday, October 11, 2003, Wayne and Tina were married in a beautiful ceremony at Immanuel Lutheran Church in Mankato. It was indeed a family wedding with the best man, ushers, and service speaker all brothers of the bride and groom. Tina's "sister" from childhood, Beth (nee Myers) Wolter, was the matron of honor. Wayne's

older brother, Michael, gave the wedding address and Pastor Paul D. Nolting officiated the rest of the ceremony. The congregation's choirs, including the Church Choir, the High School Choir, and the Children's Choir all sang during the service. The marriage address was based on Matthew 6:33, a Bible passage very near and dear to my heart. It was the passage I had personally chosen for my confirmation verse.

Seek ye first the kingdom of God,
and his righteousness;
and all these things shall be
added unto you.

The whole congregation was invited to the wedding reception at the Civic Center in Mankato. Tina's cousins, all

Wayne and Tina
on their Wedding Day (2003)

three sons of her godparents, Ed and Verona Lentz, and their spouses were the hosts and hostesses for their reception. My daughter wanted me to be a mother of the bride and as such *not* carry a camera or take pictures during the day and evening. She knew what she was doing, of course, as I *love* to take pictures, especially of such wonderful occasions. But I listened to her and did not carry a camera. Fortunately, a friend had taken some pictures of the cake and one of the three food spots, each one with a different type of meal for guests to choose from. It was an enchanting event. There were close to 600 people in attendance. Thank You, Lord, for adding the gift of this special *son-in-love* to our family.

One week later, on Saturday, October 18, 2003, Neal and Erin

were married in a beautiful ceremony at Messiah Lutheran Church in Eau Claire. Pastor Paul Tiefel Jr. married them. He had confirmed Erin and encouraged Neal into the ministry. Once again it was truly a family wedding with the service speaker, best man, maid of honor, two bridesmaids, a groomsman, one of the musicians, and most of the vocalists being immediate family members of the bride or groom. My brother Jim, Neal's uncle, did the wedding address, which he was excited about doing, since he had never preached on their chosen verse at a wedding before. The wedding text chosen was Ecclesiastes 4:9-12 with the theme:

Neal and Erin
on their Wedding Day (2003)

Two are better than one—
Three is best of all!

The reception was held at the Quality Inn in Eau Claire, the same place we had the groom's dinner for the wedding rehearsal the night before. Since I was a *guest* at the wedding, I carried a camera and took a few pictures. Thank You, Lord, for the gift of another special *daughter-in-love* to our family.

Before Wayne and Tina were married, they had purchased a house in Mankato where they would be living after their marriage. It was a lovely split entry home. Neal and Erin lived in an apartment for a year after they got married after which they found a split entry home in Eau Claire, which included an outdoor pool. It was fun to visit both couples in their new homes.

We had thought about giving both couples a cruising honeymoon as a wedding gift, but Wayne and Tina had already decided on going to New Zealand for their honeymoon, which they did. Neal and Erin, however, did enjoy a western Caribbean cruise on Carnival's ship *Inspiration* for their honeymoon. Then three years later, Wayne and Tina finally took their cruise on the inside passage to Alaska on Carnival's ship *Spirit*, which they enjoyed.

In 2007, Jeff was finishing up his college life when he attended the wedding of his friend, Chad Seybt. There he met Sarah Noeldner, who was a friend of Chad. Jeff had not been at ILC when Sarah attended, so there was no overlap in their high school days. BUT he said he remembered exactly what she was wearing at the wedding!

In the summer of 2008, he graduated from the Carlson School of Management with an MBA while still working at Graco as a Global Product Marketing Manager. By April 2008, Jeff and Sarah were dating. Then in June Sarah got sick and by July was in the hospital in Eau Claire with probable Behcet's disease, a rare Middle Eastern autoimmune disease. At one point Sarah's parents, Tim and Lisa, came to see her in the hospital while Jeff was there with her. Jeff had been told by the nurse that Sarah was supposed to sleep and shouldn't be disturbed. When Lisa tried to go into Sarah's room, Jeff stopped her and said she couldn't go in. Lisa told Jeff, "She's my daughter!" But Jeff said, "No, you still can't go in. She's supposed to rest." Jeff was already watching out for this wonderful girl with whom he had fallen in love. By August, Jeff had proposed to Sarah at her parents' home.

On Saturday, October 3, 2008, Jeff and Sarah were married in a beautiful ceremony at Messiah Lutheran Church in Eau Claire. They held their reception in the church fellowship hall with Mark and Trudy Wales as the host and hostess. All the siblings of Jeff and Sarah were involved in the ceremony in some way. The wedding text was chosen from Joshua 24:15:

Jeff and Sarah
on their Wedding Day (2008)

As for me and my house,
we will serve the LORD.

And once again, we thank the Lord for adding the gift of a special *daughter-in-love* to our family.

During Jeff's time at Graco, he had also done a lot of traveling. For their honeymoon, we gave them a week's trip to Greece, where they had decided they wanted to go. It was truly a blessing from the Lord for us to be able to do this for them as we were able to do for the other children.

We now had three God-given *daughters-in-love* and one *son-in-love*. The first time I heard that term "in love" was from Rena Tarbet, a Mary Kay national sales director, at a seminar in Dallas. She said she didn't like the term "in law" as it always seemed to carry a bad connotation. She preferred to say *daughter-in-love* for the love her son had for his wife when he married her. I totally agreed in my heart with Rena and ever since then I have been using the term "in-love" with each one of these gifts. To God be the glory!

> The mercy of the LORD is from everlasting to
> everlasting upon them that fear him,
> and his righteousness unto children's children.
> Psalm 103:17

In April of 2009, I took a trip with my four daughters to Washington, DC, a place I had always wanted to see. Erin flew to Minneapolis from California where they were living. Tina drove to Minneapolis from Mankato, while Sarah already lived in the Minneapolis area where we were. We boarded a plane for DC together to start our trip. While we were flying to DC, I was concerned about Tina who was seven months pregnant with her second child. At this time Erin announced to us that she too was expecting a child, her third, in December. Now I had two daughters to pray about on this flight to DC. Meanwhile, Leigh was flying directly to Washington, DC from Atlanta and we met her at the airport there. For five days this vacation was a true bonding time for the sisters and especially joyful for me to watch them bond.

During the five days we were there, we saw just about everything we could from Arlington National Cemetery to the Iwo Jima Memorial, to the World War II Memorial, to the White House, to Union Station, to the Capitol, the Library of Congress, Ford's Theater/Peterson House, and the John F. Kennedy Center for the Performing Arts where we watched *Ragtime* in the Eisenhower Theater. We ate at many fun and good food places, but the seafood at The Wharf stands out in my mind—I love lobster! Then on Sunday, April 26, 2009, we took the Metro to the Old Town Hall building in Fairfax, Virginia to attend church at our sister congregation which was there at the time. Pastor Glenn Oster, Erin's uncle, was the minister. There was a confirmation during the service which made it even more special to us as we could each remember our own confirmations, which for me had been fifty years earlier.

After the service, Pastor Oster took us to the Metro where we had to scurry back to the hotel, check out, and get to our planes. We left Leigh at one gate for her flight back to Georgia as we went on to our gate to go back to Minnesota. What a very special trip this had been for all of us, especially for me as I had hoped to see Washington, DC for many years but to do it with my daughters was even more special! Thank You, Lord, for this bonding time for the women of our family.

During the next year, the girls secretly made a very large scrapbook of our trip and on the last few pages, each one had written a letter to me about all the fun times we had and what they had especially enjoyed. As I looked through all the pages and then read each letter on the back pages, my eyes were full of tears. When we started the trip, I said I was going to write a poem at the end of each day, so I had something to remember about the trip. I did not get that done during the trip. So, after receiving this heartfelt treasure from them, I sat down and wrote my poems for each day using the pages in the book as my inspiration for it. I then wrote this letter to the girls on April 13, 2010, thanking them for their special surprise they had worked so hard on.

After they received this email from me, they added six pages to the back of the book which included this letter plus a page for each of the five poems I wrote—one for each day of the trip. Thank You, Lord, for my daughters!

4-13-2010

My dear Daughters,

You are all such a blessing to me! As I look back at the pictures in this fantastic book you have put together, I am amazed at how much we actually did in a relatively short time. If I never get back to DC, it won't matter – YOU all made the first time the BEST time!

Then I reread your letters again and the tears flow! God has so richly blessed Dad and I with awesome children who have truly been blessed by that same God in finding awesome mates 'fit' for each of them. No parents could ask for anything more. Your love of Christ comes through your letters and touches my heart so deeply.

It has been one year since our trip. My goal to write a poem for each day is finally complete. Yes, Tina, I am crossing it off my 'Bucket List.' ☺ I had hoped to write these at the end of each day (which I did the first day) but was surprisingly too tired to do each of the following days.

I continue to thank our LORD that both Anna and Jason survived the 'trip' to join Tyler, Alex, Titus, Caleb, and Gabi at our family reunions. God is good and gracious.

I love you all dearly – but Jesus loves you more.

Jesus keep you,
Mom, Mom R, Mommer, Jackie, Grandma, Gama

Special Thoughts for a Special Gift from my daughters (2010)

With marriage often comes the blessing of offspring. At this point in my writing, we have ten such blessings of the Lord. Each grandchild is a joy to their parents as a gift from their Father in Heaven. Each grandchild has been redeemed by the washing of water and the Word. Each grandchild has Christian godparents chosen to continue to pray and to remind him or her of their baptism throughout life. Each grandchild is also a gift to their grandparents and has a special place in our hearts and prayers. Each grandchild is growing up in *"the nurture and admonition of the Lord."* To God be the glory!

On Saturday, January 11, 2003, at 10:36 a.m., **Tyler Philip Radichel** was born to Brian and Leigh Radichel in Lawrenceville, Georgia. He weighed 8 lb. 2 oz. and was 21.25". Tyler was baptized on Sunday,

January 19, 2003, by Pastor Nathanael Mayhew. His godparents are his Uncle Wayne and Aunt Tina (nee Radichel) Eichstadt. Tyler was confirmed in Dallas, Texas on Sunday, May 14, 2017, by Pastor Matthew Hanel. His confirmation passage was John 17:3.

On Monday, May 23, 2005, at 10:21 a.m., **Alexander David Radichel** was born to Brian and Leigh Radichel in Lawrenceville, Georgia. He weighed 6 lb. 13 oz. and was 19.5". Alex was baptized on Monday, May 23, 2005, by Pastor Nathanael Mayhew. His godparents are his Uncle Wayne and Aunt Tina (nee Radichel) Eichstadt. Alex was confirmed in Dallas, Texas on Sunday, June 9, 2019, by Pastor Matthew Hanel. His confirmation passage was 1 Corinthians 10:31.

On Saturday, April 1, 2006, at 1:47 a.m., **Titus Jacob Radichel** was born to Pastor Neal and Erin Radichel in Eau Claire, Wisconsin. He weighed 8 lb. 3 oz. and was 20.25". Titus was baptized on Palm Sunday, April 9, 2006, by Pastor Paul Tiefel Jr. His godparents are his Uncle Aaron and Aunt Heather (nee Oster) Thompson. Titus was confirmed in Mankato, Minnesota on Sunday, May 17, 2020, by his father, Pastor Neal Radichel. His confirmation passage was Ephesians 2:8–9.

On Friday, June 29, 2007, at 7:33 p.m., **Caleb Wayne Eichstadt** was born to Pastor Wayne and Tina Eichstadt in Mankato, Minnesota. He weighed 8 lb. 13.5 oz. and was 22.75". Caleb was baptized on Saturday, June 30, 2007, by his father, Pastor Wayne Eichstadt. His godparents are his Uncle Jeff and Aunt Sarah (nee Noeldner) Radichel. Caleb was confirmed in Spokane Valley, Washington on Sunday, June 6, 2021, by his father, Pastor Wayne Eichstadt. His confirmation passage was Jude 1:3b.

On Friday, December 28, 2007, at 1:02 a.m., **Gabrielle Christine Radichel** was born to Pastor Neal and Erin Radichel in San Jose, California. She weighed 7 lb. 12 oz. and was 19.25". Gabrielle was baptized on Sunday, January 13, 2008, by her father, Pastor Neal Radichel. Her godparent is her Aunt Megan (nee Oster) Johnston. Gabrielle was confirmed in Mankato, Minnesota on April 24, 2022, by her father, Pastor Neal Radichel. Her confirmation passage was Ephesians 2:8–9.

On Friday, June 19, 2009, at 2:45 a.m., **Anna Esther Eichstadt** was born to Pastor Wayne and Tina Eichstadt in Mankato, Minnesota. She weighed 9 lb. 6.6 oz. and was 22.5". Anna was baptized on Saturday, June 20, 2009, by her father, Pastor Wayne Eichstadt. Her godparents are her Uncle Michael and Aunt Sue (nee Pelzl) Eichstadt.

On Thursday, December 17, 2009, at 10:17 a.m., **Jason Aaron Radichel** was born to Pastor Neal and Erin Radichel in Santa Clara, California. He weighed 10 lb. 1 oz. and was 22". Jason was baptized on Thursday, Christmas Day, December 25, 2009, by his father, Pastor Neal Radichel. His godparents are his Uncle Wayne and Aunt Tina (nee Radichel) Eichstadt.

On Thursday, May 12, 2011, at 3:08 p.m., **Drew Timothy Eichstadt** was born to Pastor Wayne and Tina Eichstadt in Mankato, Minnesota. He weighed 8 lb. 13.9 oz. and was 22". Drew was baptized on Saturday, May 14, 2011, by his father, Pastor Wayne Eichstadt. His godparents are Matthew and Julie (nee Wheaton) Busch.

On Friday, October 19, 2012, at 3:27 a.m., **Levi Benjamin Radichel** was born to Pastor Neal and Erin Radichel in Fond du Lac, Wisconsin. He weighed 8 lb. 14 oz. and was 20.5". Levi was baptized on Sunday, October 28, 2012, by his father, Pastor Neal Radichel. His godparent is his Aunt Megan (nee Oster) Johnston.

On Thursday, December 26, 2013, at 3:44 p.m., **Asher Jon Eichstadt** was born to Pastor Wayne and Tina Eichstadt in Mankato, Minnesota. He weighed 9 lb. 4.4 oz. and was 21". Asher was baptized on Saturday, December 28, 2013, by his father, Pastor Wayne Eichstadt. His godparents are his Uncle Neal and Aunt Erin (nee Oster) Radichel.

Thus shall the man be blessed that feareth the LORD . . .
Yea, thou shalt see thy children's children.
Psalm 128:4,6

Oh, the joy and blessings the Lord has given us through these ten grandchildren over the years! We have watched each of them grow in the nurture and admonition of the Lord as their parents daily apply God's Word to their lives. Each child has shown and continues to show us their love in many ways through their gifts of time in creating drawings, writing letters, and personally helping us when they come to visit. I especially appreciate their loving hugs whenever we are privileged to visit with them. I love to sing to them when I can tuck them into bed and say their prayers with them, just as I did with our own children. I love to hear them play music on the piano or sing songs that they are learning or hear their latest stories about what they are doing. All generations of children are such a rich blessing from our Lord. One of the true blessings our family has enjoyed is being able to worship together wherever we are. If several of us vacation together and are not near one of our congregations, we still have our own daily devotions or Sunday worship service.

As our grandchildren grow, we are blessed to be able to participate in many of their special functions, from spiritual events and milestones to ordinary day-to-day activities such as sports events, musical events, and numerous school events. Tyler, being the oldest grandchild, was the first to begin high school in the Fall of 2017, and was excited to be able to go to his father's alma mater, Immanuel Lutheran High School in Eau Claire. Since they lived in Dallas, Brian would put him on a plane and Tyler would have a direct flight to MSP in Minneapolis, where Phil and I would pick him up and take him to Eau Claire, which was one-and-a half to two hours east, depending on the traffic and the road construction. And in this part of the country, traffic and road construction are always going on! When it would be time for him to go home for an orthodontic appointment, either we'd go get him and bring him back to the airport, or after his freshman year, he would sometimes get on the airport shuttle bus in Eau Claire, and they'd get him to the MSP airport. Tyler was always ahead of the game and could take care of himself most of the time.

Two years after Tyler started, his brother, Alex, also began at ILC so the trips were easier since both boys were usually flying together. The third grandson, Titus, began the following Fall after Alex. ILC was the alma mater for both of Titus's parents. The year Titus was to start in the Fall of 2020, we were working through the COVID-19 virus effects and beginning the reopening phase. It was an interesting time for all the grandkids as they were all doing online school from home at various times during the school year. I've always said, "I'm thankful the Lord is in charge of our lives and won't give us more than we can handle." As our fourth grandson, Caleb, has begun his high school years at ILC, which is also the alma mater of both of his parents, we are still working through the drama of COVID. We continue to *"pray without ceasing"* (1 Thessalonians 5:17)!

I so look forward to the years our Lord gives us, allowing us to participate in all our children's and grandchildren's lives as much as we can without being a burden or embarrassment to them as they grow and mature. I would like to think we can be a spiritual reminder to all of them as to why the Lord has put them on this earth and help them to see the personal gifts He has given to each of them to do His work while He has them here. With five of our grandchildren in high school or college and five more to reach that level, the next ten years will be a challenge for us just to keep up with all the forthcoming activities of the grandchildren that we so want to participate in with them. We know the work our own children with families have yet to do in continuing to bring up their own children in His Word and by His grace. We also pray for our Lord's grace in providing not only for the emotional and financial needs of all our own children, but also the special needs of those with families, as He has so richly blessed our lives while raising them. To God be the glory!

It has thus been a joy to watch our own children raising or helping to raise the next generation in our family. The cousins love to play together whenever they have the opportunity. All the aunts and uncles love to be around all the children, no matter whose kids they are. They watch out for each of them as if they are their own. Our family get-togethers thrive on togetherness, both in play and in service to our Lord. Our children grew up watching us work in the Lord's kingdom. All our children helped with those building projects we did at church and school. All our children and their spouses continue to be active in their local congregations and in synod work. The men are preachers or councilmen or convention reps or men's group and youth group organizers. Our ladies participate in the church women's groups as well as teach in our church schools or help within their congregations in many ways, even if they work in secular jobs. What a blessing it is to watch them, and even participate with them, in many of these activities, knowing that their children are also watching them—and learning. Thanks be to God who blesses all the efforts and our needs in His way and in His timing.

Unto whomsoever much is given,
of him shall be much required.
Luke 12:48

What a joy to watch God's guidance
For each child along life's way,
As He leads them to discover
With their spouse to share each day!

Oh, the blessings on each marriage
As our Lord pours out His grace,
While we watch all they've been given
And His gifts they now embrace.

Chapter 8

Our Growth as a Couple

I can do all things through Christ which strengtheneth me.

Philippians 4:13

As I pointed out earlier, I had prayed for a husband of my own faith from the time I was a small child of five until I was fifteen. I met the answer to my prayers on the steps of church, June 1960, at Our Redeemer's Lutheran Church in Red Wing, Minnesota. How appropriate that was to me to meet this man at church as it further sealed what I knew when he walked in the door—that God was bringing him to me "until death do us part." Never has anything been more clear and complete to me in all my years than that first meeting. Not only was he chosen for me, but I too was chosen for him as it would become more evident as our lives together moved forward.

My brother Jim had initiated our introduction. In his years of school at Doctor Martin Luther College (DMLC) Jim had met this family and had roomed with one of the boyfriends of Phil's sister, Becky. While Jim was at DMLC, our church body at the time had gone through a tough reckoning of the spirit and we had left that synod and had just begun anew. My parents had been involved with the start-up of this new synod, the Church of the Lutheran Confession (CLC). Although we had left the former synod a few years before, many were still coming to see the problems in the former synod and left later than we did.

Phil's parents were part of that later departing. They were now leaving the place where they had been for many years and were searching for a church in this new synod they had come to know. As God's will was shown to us, one of Phil's sisters, Margaret, had been training as a nurse in Red Wing and had heard about our church. She and her boyfriend, Ray Seeley, had been attending our services for a while and were married later. Phil's parents decided to come to Red Wing to see this new little congregation and were thinking about moving there. When they walked into church that beautiful summer day, Jim was standing on the inside steps to the church proper. I was on the top step. There were a number of people in this family that walked through that door, but my eyes went right to the back of the group and landed on this young gentleman. As my brother said "Hi" to them and then turned to introduce me to them, he said, "Jack, this is the family from Iowa that I was telling you about, the Radichels." I was so struck with seeing the answer to my prayer, I don't even remember if I said anything other than, "Hi."

Our growth as a couple began that first day we met on the steps of the church. Within the first few dates we had fallen in love and were committed to each other as a couple. We were confiding in each other and supporting each other. We have talked about that periodically in our relationship both before and after we were married. Our growth started with the scriptures to be led by God's Word in how and why we were both in this new synod. It grew to understanding what God was planning for our lives together as we were convinced He put us together for a reason. Phil once told me that he "wouldn't classify our relationship during this time as growth but more as maturity—they are not the same. You came out of confirmation class well-established on doctrine and scripture, but maturity developed during experiencing life." He was (and is) always so right in explaining things.

Then came the hard part—I had to learn all over again my worth as a child of God and not feel like the worthless child I thought myself to be. Yes, I had an inferiority complex that was so hidden inside that it took years for my boyfriend, and then husband, to show me how a child of God should feel. For a year and a half after meeting and then until several dates into our relationship as a couple, I hid it from everyone I knew. Most people thought I was an outgoing, happy person without a care in the world. But as our dating continued, this special man in my life saw through all my shields and got into my real soul. Many date nights were turned into crying sessions as we talked about who I was and how I felt about high school, my friends, my family, my secrets, and my attitude on everything. This young man was indeed sent by God to help me through the darkest moments of my youth. Thank You, Lord, for knowing my needs and giving me this special person to bring me closer to You!

Although it took a whole year for our relationship to develop into a couple, the next five years of our actual dating brought continual growth in our fellowship with our God and our families. We spent a lot of time with family members, both individually and as a couple. I enjoyed the friendship of Phil's sister, Lydia, with whom I was very close—she was like my own sister. I even asked her to be my maid of honor at our wedding. With the Christian home and parochial school education I grew up with, I so appreciated the reasons that Phil's family went out of their way to move out of the tight-knit family community they had in Iowa to search out a congregation that held to the true Word of God. As I continued to watch the hand of the Lord, I was amazed at the blessings that continued to come my way.

Phil and I had a lot of fun with our parents. Mine were like our best friends, even more than people of our own age. Part of this was due to the cabin. Another part was because, after we had children, they came and took care of our kids when we had things we were supposed to do. As for Phil's parents, we helped them build houses. We also took the big trip around Lake Superior with them, along with Brian and Tina when they were small. I recall the fun time we had during that trip at Mackinaw Island when we took a tour of the island entitled, "Furry with the Syringe on Top." The tour's story was based on the actual carriage we rode in called a surrey (that had a fringe on top).

As a couple, we also spent a lot of time with Jim and Carol whenever we had an opportunity to do so, before and after marriage. Jim was studying for the ministry and Carol was studying to be a Christian Day School teacher. If we had a day the four of us could get together, we'd take rides along the Mississippi River to Maiden Rock, Wisconsin, or drive to Mankato, Minnesota to see other friends. Our family relationship between the four of us grew steadily throughout our dating as it was blessed by our Lord. We confided in each other spiritually as well as individually, Carol and I, as well as Jim and Phil. Even our weddings were blessed by the relationship we had spiritually. Jim and Carol were married first, and I was Carol's personal attendant. Eight weeks later Phil and I were married. Carol was my personal attendant and Jim, who had just been ordained, married us. We were now *officially* as well as *spiritually* family. Thank You, Lord!

> *If any would not work, neither should he eat.*
> *2 Thessalonians 3:10b*

The Lord had seen fit to grant us not only the ability to work, but also the jobs that provided greatly for our livelihood. Phil was promoted up the ranks in his work as I was in mine. We knew we would want to be able to give our children the benefits of a stay-at-home

Mom as well as give them a Christian education from grade school through high school and that we needed to begin saving toward these goals. When work nights got late or out-of-town travel interrupted our daily routines, we always knew there was a purpose for it and each of us would do our best to help the other through it.

Church work became very important to us as our church life always was, and had been, to each of our families. After our marriage in 1966, we joined our CLC church in the Minneapolis area, Grace Lutheran Church in Fridley, Minnesota. Even though we still went to Red Wing often, Grace was now our church home. The church and parsonage were combined into one facility. You could come in the front door of the parsonage and go either into the parsonage itself or into the church proper, or you could come in the church front door itself. The basement of the church was a walkout to the church parking lot and included a fellowship hall for any church functions. Later, that basement also held the Christian Day School that was started at Grace. We had a small church membership, and everyone knew each other. It has always been a spiritually warm congregation of believers.

Phil became a voter right away after we joined and has served in many roles in the church council at Grace as well as being a delegate to our synod conventions. In 1980 during our CLC Convention in Eau Claire, Wisconsin, a major storm took down many trees on the campus of ILC where the Convention was being held. Fortunately, no one was hurt. My parents were there because my dad was a member of the CLC Board of Trustees and had been since the CLC started in 1960. I had not gone to the Convention this time when Phil went the day before, so I decided to ride along with one of our Grace members who was going over to help clean up the debris on the campus. While I was out clearing brush, someone came out during a break to see how all of us were doing on the cleanup. He came over to me and said, "Well, your dad got his wish. After twenty years he is no longer on the Board of Trustees—but your husband is." Thus began thirty-six years of Phil being on the CLC Board of Trustees, most of them as chairman.

In the early 1980s, Grace had grown in numbers and the members wanted to build a bigger church. We had welcomed a new pastor to our congregation, Pastor Daniel Fleischer and his wife Barbara and their three children. We remodeled the former chapel area into a larger home for this family. We became close friends with them over the years. I also did some secretarial work for Pastor during this time. As it turned out, we see them a lot since they too had married in 1966, as we had, and became part of our "anniversary group" of friends who had married this same year. Even now, their daughter, Janelle, who is married to our current pastor John Hein, is back living in the same home we worked on when she was a young girl.

The school was also growing, and space was getting tight. Phil and I helped to build this new church building, which was attached to the parsonage but on the other side of it. We helped tear out parts of the old church building and remake the former church into more parsonage space for our pastor's family. Our children were growing up during this time and spent time with us at church doing some work as they were able. Jeff and Neal were still young when we started so some of the teenage girls would keep an eye on them for me. The work progressed for several years and was blessed by the Lord with congeniality between the members working together for a common goal.

After twenty years of marriage, Phil and I were entering a new phase of our personal growth in learning how to become caregivers to our parents. In 1986, while working on building a new porch on our home, my dad was helping Phil wire the porch and put in the electrical cords. It was getting toward suppertime and Dad rolled up the end of the cord, threw it in between the studs, and said to Phil, "I'm done working on this. We need to head home." They left the next morning. A couple of days later, Mom called to tell me she had taken Dad to the hospital in Detroit Lakes, Minnesota. It seems he had a heart attack, and they were going to transfer him to the hospital in Fargo, North Dakota. Of course, I dropped everything, got in the car, and drove straight to Detroit Lakes. My dear husband was left to care for the children, still go to work, and get any friends or family to help him. He did a wonderful job of being a caring husband and father during the week I was with my dad at the hospital.

Meanwhile, I had called my brother Jim who then drove from Coloma, Michigan, where he was serving a congregation, to Fargo to be with Mom and me. When I got to Detroit Lakes, I picked up Mom and went to Fargo. Dad was semiconscious, with a ventilator and an IV, and was not able to talk. I sat with him on and off along with Mom. When Jim got there, we took turns either to be with Mom or to be with Dad. At one time I was alone with Dad, and he was motioning to say something. I suddenly thought of getting a piece of paper and a pen so he could write. He wrote, "Where's Phil?" I was crushed. I knew Phil had to work and someone had to take care of the kids, but I felt so bad that he couldn't be here when Dad wanted him. I had been told that Dad wasn't expected to live much longer and now he wouldn't be able to see Phil. I told him Phil was working and he nodded, seemingly understanding the situation. Then he wrote, "The bills." I told him I was taking care of it. With that, he put the pen and paper down and went back to sleep. Later Jim wanted to know if we should go back to the house so Mom could get some sleep. I asked him to take her and said that I wanted to stay all night. He and Mom left.

At one point I called Dad's doctor in Minneapolis and told him what was going on. He asked if he could speak to the doctor taking care of Dad, who happened to be at the desk at the nursing station. I gave the phone to the doctor and when he was done talking to Dad's Minneapolis doctor, he handed the phone back to me. Dad's doctor then said to me, "The man's whole anterior portion of his heart is gone, he can't live!" I thanked him for telling me straight out and told him I'd talk to him later.

That night I spent most of the night in Dad's room somewhat awake. At one point I was standing in the doorway to his room, leaning against the doorjamb. Suddenly I jumped as I felt someone standing in front of me. It was a nurse or a doctor—I don't remember if there was one or two of them. They said I was asleep standing up and they were afraid I was going to fall. I asked if Dad was gone, and they said no he wasn't. I went back to the chair to sleep for a while. When morning came, Jim was going to bring Mom back. I told him I was going to go home that day. It was Friday and Phil's godchild, Tom Lentz, was going to be married the next day, and I wanted to be at the wedding. After Jim and Mom got to the hospital, I left to go home.

On the way back to Minneapolis, since I hadn't had much sleep, I could feel myself falling asleep a few times just before I got to St. Cloud. I stopped at the first restaurant I found and went up to the counter and told the hostess I needed a quart Styrofoam container filled three quarters full of hot water for tea and to bring me three tea bags. She looked at me funny and said, "Are you okay?" I said, "Yes, just please bring it to me." She did. I took the three tea bags and dipped them up and down in the hot water until the water was very dark. Then I threw those in the waste can and asked her to fill the container with ice to cool the water down. I paid her for three cups of tea and as I left to go out, she asked me again, "Are you sure you're okay?" I assured her I just needed to have some tea and left. All the rest of the way home I drank the tea to stay awake. When I walked in the door, I needed to go to the bathroom immediately, of course, and as I went down the hall, Phil told me that very shortly after I left, Dad had died. Then the tears flowed. Still, I knew Daddy believed in his Lord and therefore I knew where he was. His passing was on Friday, October 3, 1986.

Surely goodness and mercy shall follow me all the days of my life: and I will dwell in the house of the LORD for ever.
Psalm 23:6

We did go to the wedding the next day, but I didn't want to interrupt the joy of the day and tried to stay in the background. I didn't want to hug anyone in case it would bring tears again. The Lord had taken Daddy when I wasn't there, but I knew where He was taking him and that gave me peace.

The victory service for Charles Henry Sandeen was held at Our Redeemer's Lutheran Church in Red Wing on Tuesday, October 7, 1986. He was laid to rest with a committal service in Oakview Cemetery in Red Wing. His grandchildren sang "Children of the Heavenly Father" at this service. Thank You, Lord! Hallelujah!

After my dad died, we moved into a caregiving role with my mom until she died. Dad had been commenting that he thought that Mom was forgetting things. We decided she should sell the house in Detroit Lakes and move to the Twin Cities where I could take care of her. Jim agreed with that since, as a pastor, he could be moving around from time to time and that wouldn't be good for her. Besides, he would be a long way from her in Michigan and not be able to help her much. It didn't take long to move her things to our house and to get hers sold. We threw away a lot of things before the move that she didn't want or need.

Mom stayed with us for several months. We did notice her forgetfulness and memory issues. Before one of her doctor appointments, I was telling her doctor privately about my concerns. His comment was, "And where will your children be when she doesn't remember to turn off the kitchen stove and starts a fire in the house?" Shortly after that conversation, Phil and I decided that she needed to move into a safer environment. We moved her into a seniors' apartment complex within two miles of our house, called Chardon Court, where Phil's parents had also recently moved. She could drive to our house easily, for a while, until we finally had to take her car away from her after she had gotten lost one time.

It was about this time, in the late 1980s, that I began thinking about being able to work outside the home again. As a medical technologist, my husband and I had waited six years after we were married to start our family so I could get my professional career established. After we had our first child, I quit as assistant chief technologist at North Memorial Medical Center to be a full-time mom. Four children and many volunteer projects later, as we were contemplating our finances for our college-bound children, I told my husband that I should go back to work again. I reminded him that I did not want to work weekends since that was our only family time and that I needed a set hour in the morning and another in the afternoon to drive our children to school. I didn't know what I could do to work around that schedule.

Out of the blue Phil said, "Why don't you do Mary Kay?" I said, "What?" He reminded me that I had been using the products for a while and how much I liked them. He also reminded me how much I loved working with people. "Besides," he said, "you'd be good at it!" So, since I *always* do what my husband tells me to do, I called my Mary Kay consultant, Lonna Andolshek, who later became my director, and asked her what I had to do to get into Mary Kay. She said, "What?" So, I became a Mary Kay consultant and later a Mary Kay director myself. Now after more than thirty-three years, I still love the product, the flexibility, and the income. I work when I want and as much as I want, but I know I always have a job which I enjoy doing, and I still love the people.

By the fall of 1990, I had been concerned enough about Mom's memory that I investigated increased memory care and got her into the Medicare Alzheimer's Research Project. We also moved her from Chardon Court to North Ridge Care Center just a couple of blocks down from Chardon Court. She was in the senior care area for a while. At one time the staff asked me what they could do to keep her busy as they found her trying to take care of other residents. She had tried to help one lady get to the toilet by lifting her out of her wheelchair—and then couldn't get her to the toilet so Mom had dropped her on the floor. That ended that situation!

They then moved Mom to the memory care unit. I mentioned to the staff there that Mom loved to help so why didn't they give her clean kitchen towels to fold for them. I suggested that after she folded them up and they thanked her dearly for doing that, they should take the towels back to the kitchen, shake them out, put them back in the basket, and take them back to her to fold. She would never know they were the same towels and would always feel like she was helping them. They were amazed at how many times in one morning Mom was willing to fold the same towels over and over again. Even better, Mom was so happy to be helping them.

After a couple of more years in the memory care unit and being part of the Medicare Alzheimer's Research Project, Mom's overall health was failing her. It got to the point where she didn't know me and was also bedridden. I would go into her room and moisturize her very dry skin with my wonderful Mary Kay skin care products, and she would "oooh" and "aaah" because it felt so good. Then she would say to me, "Thank you so much lady, would you come back tomorrow and do that again?" I just said, "OK" and would leave for the day. I was glad she was comfortable and knew she was always in the Lord's hands. In His time and in His way, He would take care of her until He was ready to take her home to Him.

I cried a lot during those times which, of course, was hormone related at that time in my life. But the Lord had kept us busy enough which helped us focus on other things that were important at the time. He gave us children, parents to take care of, building a church, and working for the CLC. We learned to deal with a lot—through prayer! Thank You, Lord!

In His time and in His way, the Lord took care of Mom by releasing her from her earthly trials and taking her to her place in Heaven on Sunday, June 12, 1994. It happened while we were attending church. When we got home from church, there was a voicemail on our phone saying that I should call North Ridge. When I called, they said I should come immediately to the care center. I asked if Mom had already died, and they said she had. I told them I would be over shortly.

The victory service for Rosa Anna Elsie (Schmidt) Sandeen was held at Grace Lutheran Church in Fridley on Wednesday, June 15, 1994. After the funeral, her casket was driven to Red Wing where there was a graveside service in Oakwood Cemetery, and she was laid to rest next to her husband. Her grandchildren sang "Children of the Heavenly Father" at this service. Oh, what peace, what joy in watching the hand of the Lord once again in our lives!

In my Father's house are many mansions: if it were not so, I would have told you. I go to prepare a place for you. And if I go and prepare a place for you, I will come again, and receive you unto myself; that where I am, there ye may be also.
John 14: 2–3

As we've journeyed through our lifetime,
Each phase blessed by God's rich grace,
He has giv'n us many missions
As we moved from place to place.

We've been richly blessed with children,
Helped our parents as they aged,
Bonded more with each experience
As life turned from page to page.

Chapter 9

Our Final Years

To every thing there is a season,
and a time to every purpose under the heaven.

Ecclesiastes 3:1

We are now in our final years as a couple, that is over age seventy-five and celebrating more than fifty-five years of marriage, I find the biggest struggle we have in life is to cut back on the amount of time and effort we put forth in the work of the church. This is very hard for me not only to do, but to allow my husband to do as well. We have both grown up in families that totally supported the work of the church as well as the pastor and his family, whether it was in building projects, teaching others, helping to feed the pastor and his family, attending meetings, singing in the choir, or serving on a board of the synod.

I have talked about my father and his spiritual growth. I watched him become weary with the work as he approached his seventies. He used to comment about the youth of the church, wondering when they were going to step up to take on some of this work. When Phil was elected in Dad's place to the Board of Trustees for the synod in

1980, Dad so appreciated and enjoyed watching Phil's maturity on the board over the next few years. Dad was always willing to offer Phil his time to commiserate and work through any issues Phil would have and provide background on the issues as well. Phil and Dad had a loving, father/son relationship that was such a joy to me.

When Phil decided to step down from his responsibilities on the Board of Trustees after thirty-six years, he was still concerned about the work and willing to offer his assistance and experience to who-ever took his place as chairman. He has continued working on synod computer software since then, which not many people realize, since he does most of it from home. When Phil quit working full-time for Enteromedics in a routine capacity in 2015, he began to do consulting work around the upper Midwest. We both enjoyed that as we traveled to different places, mostly by car, and got to be together and still feel like we were on a vacation. He did that for several years.

One of the hardest things for me to step down from was singing in choir. Phil had been ready to stop for several years, but he was a bass and there was only one other bass, at most, occasionally singing with him. I was losing my voice and not able to sing the higher notes as well as I used to, which bothered me personally. Because I was also very loud when I sang, it certainly was not appropriate for me to be in the choir singing both poorly and then loudly besides. Others did step up to both positions, which we were thankful for, since we do love to hear the choir sing.

I also have worked my Mary Kay business for more than thir-ty-three years and love the product and the people I have met along the way. My family has often suggested I stop working as a consultant so I can do other things I want to do in life, like finish this book, but I love the product so much for myself, and I do love the people—they are like family to me. My business has also given me many opportu-nities to share God's Word with others, help people who are dealing with life's tragedies, and be an example of living in thankfulness to my Lord for all His blessings as His child. To God be the glory!

In our marriage, Phil and I have traveled to many places, not only within the U.S., including Alaska and Hawaii, but also to Europe and the Bahamas. We had the short but memorable trip to Scotland to see Jeff when he was there for a semester of school at the University of Edinburgh. We also went to Austria and Germany with Jeff and Sarah where I sang "The Sound of Music" from the top of the hill (a life-time dream for me) and got to drive on the Autobahn at 160 mph/235 kph—that was interesting! Later we went back to France and Italy with them on a different trip, where we explored lots of ancient cities and toured wineries, compliments of Sarah.

In the early 1990s, we took an excursion trip to the Bahamas where we signed up for a vacation club which we still use to this day. We have had many personal family reunions of our immediate family in various resorts and have enjoyed the time with our children and grandchildren. Now as these grandkids are growing up, we can do more things with them and enjoy watching the parents parenting them, while the aunts and uncles spoil them! I still like to rub their backs, run my fingers through their hair, and sing to them at any time during the day or at night. Since each family lives in a different town, we get to visit all of our children wherever they are and enjoy our time together as adults.

On a larger scale, the Radichel Reunions bring many families to-gether from Phil's side of the family. We can get from forty to ninety people at the reunions with all age ranges. We play games, play golf, picnic, and hang out together. What a joy it is to reminisce about days gone by and things coming up. It's such a joy to watch all the children and many of the following generations grow and mature in His grace.

These later years of life allow for more direct contact with our friends of old. We continue to enjoy our group wedding gatherings that we have tried to have every five years with the five couples who all got married in 1966, but we are now down to four couples. We have tried to get together even more often in these later years as time allows. Our connections have all been from high school days or as family. We have been kept together by church work and family gatherings which entwine our fellowship even closer. And now that we all live within a hundred miles of each other, we can take day trips to be together. Besides Phil and me, the other couples are my brother, Jim, and his wife Carol, Dan and Barb Fleischer, John and Sharon Schierenbeck, and Mike and Kathy Sydow. Two years before our forty-fifth wedding anniversary, Mike was in the hospital with pancreatic cancer. Because of his condition, the four couples had dinner together and then went to see Mike and Kathy. We were all so thankful that we got together one more time as the Lord took Mike home just three-and-a-half months later. Thank You, Lord, for the fellowship of this faithful minister of Your Gospel.

Well done, thou good and faithful servant.
Matthew 25:21

In these later days, one occasionally looks back and wonders what could have been done differently in life to help others, whether in the jobs where one worked, or even in raising one's children. As is generally known in my immediate family, I tend to save a lot of things that most people would, or should, throw away. Little things that meant a lot at the time but added clutter as time went on. There are many items, though, I am glad I saved as they help in my personal joy to remember good things that happened. The memories uplift my heart now many years later. One of the items I saved was a letter I wrote in 2014 to our eight children—yes eight, our four and their spouses, whom I so appreciate and adore as my *children-in-love!* Here is the letter:

Dear Ones,

I don't know if I can say what my heart is thinking in a few words or not . . . but I will try.

I have had many phone conversations today, some of which were with several of you, our children. Neal's sermon last Sunday in San Francisco at St. Stephen was about the *Five Love Languages*, which most of you, if not all of you, know about. He had included the test for what type each individual has personally, and I had just taken it, finally, before Dad came home. So, after supper, without showing what I had done, I gave the test to Dad, and he willingly answered the questions. It turns out that we both have basically the same main type of Love Language, although the secondary for each of us is different. We were discussing the many blessings we have as a couple, a parent, a grandparent, and so on. We love the ways love is shown to each of us but affirmation of the job we do takes a big precedence over a gift given for the job we do.

We were also discussing how you can trust in God when He tells you He is always with you even if you can't see His blessings in what you do in your day-to-day activities. We commented how our trust should always be unconditional, knowing that He will bless our labors whether we see it

God's promises fulfilled in the beauty of His rainbow (2014)

Gradations of color show His majesty! (2014)

or not. We need to just believe it! Then the sun suddenly shone through from the West and was filtering between the trees and the light rain. As I reached for something across the table, my eyes were drawn to the eastern sky where a BIG, beautiful rainbow was presenting itself. I ran for the camera! I am attaching a couple of the pictures I took in the light rain from the back deck. It doesn't do the rainbow justice but use your imagination to brighten the colors at least ten times for the glorious colors that were there in that rainbow. And check out the penumbra as well.

And what does that rainbow say to us? It is God's promise to never again send a flood to kill all the people on this earth. It is HIS reminder that He keeps His promises so that we should know when He says He is always with us, He is! And He continues to send us His blessings whether we can recognize them or not!

I'm not apologizing for my reaction to all of this in any way. Furthermore, as I came into my office to type this email to you, I opened my email to find a letter from Marion Fitschen, who works at the Red Wing Area Chamber of Commerce. Here is what it said:

> "Jackie,
>   We just had a couple here visiting. I saw in the guest book that they were from Plymouth, so I asked whether he knew Phil & Jackie Radichel. He said, 'Oh yes, Phil was an engineer for me at Honeywell.' He said his brother also worked there—I said that would be Frank. He said they were both smart guys, worked hard and were very nice. I agreed with that. I just thought I would share that bit of information with you. It's always nice to hear good things about those we care about.
>   Marion"

Now you must know that our primary Love Language was Quality Time—a no-brainer that you all would guess of us. My secondary language was Physical Touch, which is also a no-brainer for all you that know me so well. Dad's on the other hand was Acts of Service. He worked hard during those years at Honeywell and helped many people. This man whom Marion met appreciated it and, out of the blue, Dad was reminded how hard he had worked there, and especially those times with no sleep, he would literally pray himself through the night to complete a project. Even if Marion can't tell us who this was, Dad is feeling better knowing that what he did do, not only was accomplished with prayer, but was appreciated. I find the hand of the Lord working today in answering prayers we have for several of you and reminding us that our work is not in vain. Whether we see the blessings from day to day, we need to remember that God is there with us all along the way in whatever we do.

Our prayer for all of you is that you daily remember you are in God's hands, and He is taking care of you regardless of your even thinking about it. His blessings are many for each of us. We may not see them today, but they are there—believe it!

Jesus keep you all in that Love that He gives to each of us. Pray, Praise, and Give Thanks to Him for His Love for us.

In thankfulness to our Lord for each of you and what you mean to us and the blessings we have in and through you,

Mom/Mommer/Jackie
In God We Trust

Since I had tucked this printed email in a folder to be used in this book, I hadn't read it until now. It literally brings tears to my eyes to read it again knowing that it was special to my husband, to be reminded how he was appreciated both at work by his manager and also by Marion, who took the time during her busy workday to pass on this accolade to him. My letter also pointed out to me that I have over the years tried to keep up with reminding all my children and grandchildren that God does keep His promises and is daily watching over each and every one of us. It was also another reminder to our children that we continue to pray for all of them and how blessed we are by each of them. To God be the glory!

When I brought up this whole thought of our final years with Phil, and asked him what his thoughts were, his first comment was, "We haven't slowed down!" He said it was just different because he wasn't going to work an eight hour shift every day. Our traveling during our years together wasn't as much recreation as it was work related, friends-to-see travel, or helping to move kids from one place to another. Compared to either of our parents, we have done a lot of traveling, while compared to our children, we haven't done much traveling at all.

I also asked Phil about mentoring, which I felt we were doing now during our retirement years. His comments were: "I wouldn't call it mentoring but giving advice. We've been giving advice to our kids since they were little. Different kinds of advice, but it's still the same idea. As for mentoring, you do more than I do, especially with people through your Mary Kay work. You're the support system for a lot of people. That's a fundamental difference between our two personalities. I don't give emotional support like you do. People call to tell you all about their lives; they don't do that to me."

I reminded him that I don't mind when people just need someone to talk to. I reminded him that he held his mother's hand when she needed emotional support when all his sisters had gone off to high school and he was the oldest at home. Phil thought she was having a nervous breakdown at the time. He laughed and said, "I think that was more physical support, not mental, to keep her from falling out of bed!" And then he laughed again. I said, "Call it what you want, but she needed you to be there during that particular time of her life, and you were." God puts each of us in the right place at the right time for His purpose in our lives.

Then I asked Phil if he thought there were any things in our lifetime, before or after we met, that he would call "lessons learned." He said, "No life-altering experiences. But lessons learned every day— that's a major blessing! And if you think how we have been blessed, that must come to the top of the list. Think about it . . . you made the decision to quit work, nobody made it for you. I never got laid off or lost a job—think of that as a blessing. You had some cancer that turned out minor, and I had some insignificant cancer. We've never been sick. Sure, I had some heart issues, but that's part of getting old. Nothing that was major! The incidents along the way the Lord takes care of for His children—daily reminders He wants them to grow with." Hence, we had spiritual growth as our lessons were learned in our lives.

Since these thoughts were expressed, Phil has had bypass heart surgery and a pacemaker put in. I have had a total hysterectomy after finding a bit of cancer again. It has been a trying time for both of us. Of course, you could now call that major, and certainly part of getting older, but through it all our dear Lord has been with us and continues to keep us in His care. Spiritual growth never stops. The more you go through life, dealing with life's issues, the more you can watch the hand of the Lord in everything.

And now as I come to the end of writing this book, I am once again humbled by the life the Lord has given to us. He has allowed us to be born to special parents who, in their own way and time, brought us up *"in the nurture and admonition of the Lord"* (Ephesians 6:4b). He has answered the prayer of my childhood and has given me the man He chose for me. *"Pray without ceasing"* (I Thessalonians 5:17). He said to *"be fruitful and multiply"* and blessed our marriage with children and grandchildren who all believe in their Lord and Savior (Genesis 1:28). Through all of this I can always hear Him say:

Lo, I am with you always, even unto the end of the world. Amen.
Matthew 28:20b

Now as I close upon this book
Which shares the life God gave me,
I'm reminded of His blessings
Many of which I could see.

Each one lives a life he chooses,
While this should not be ignored,
Just remember each day to be
"Watching the hand of the Lord!"

Watching the Hand of the Lord

Chapter 1: Our Parents

Born to parents God had chosen,
Their examples trained us well.
By God's Word their lives were fashioned,
In His grace we learned to dwell.

As we grew in His protection,
As we watched our parents live,
And their labors for His kingdom
From their heart and soul would give.

Chapter 2: Our Childhood

Though poor at birth we started life,
Our Lord for us had His plan.
Phil learned the joy of serving God,
Helping out his fellow man.

On Mother's knee I learned to sing,
"Jesus loves me! This I know."
And for my father she would pray
That his Savior God would show.

Chapter 3: Our Courtship

Seeking first our God's righteousness
While knowing He cares for us,
When we watch His hand in our lives,
We have so much to discuss.

The relationship we cherished
With our Father up above,
Brought our pathways close together
Helping to mature our love.

Chapter 4: Our Marriage

Oh, the joy of Your rich blessings
As we join as man and wife.
May You always keep us faithful
To Your Word throughout our life.

For the work that You've allowed us,
For Your grace along our way,
You have giv'n us rich abundance
And we thank You every day.

Chapter 5: Our Early Family Life

Born and raised in light of Scripture
Seeking first the Word of God;
Then to raise those whom God gives us
Brings to mind the roads we've trod.

Looking back at our beginnings
Where He took us on our way,
Gave us insight how to parent
Those He gave us day by day.

Chapter 6: Our Children's Education and Work Lives

As we watched each child develop
Practicing what they had learned,
Using all their God-giv'n talents,
Leaving no stone still unturned,

Many prayers we uttered daily
For their safety and their needs,
Asking God to give direction
To their issues and their needs.

Chapter 7: Our Children Mature

What a joy to watch God's guidance
For each child along life's way,
As He leads them to discover
With their spouse to share each day!

Oh, the blessings on each marriage
As our Lord pours out His grace,
While we watch all they've been given
And His gifts they now embrace.

Chapter 8: Our Growth as a Couple

As we've journeyed through our lifetime,
Each phase blessed by God's rich grace,
He has giv'n us many missions
As we moved from place to place.

We've been richly blessed with children,
Helped our parents as they aged,
Bonded more with each experience
As life turned from page to page.

Chapter 9: Our Final Years

Now as I close upon this book
Which shares the life God gave me,
I'm reminded of His blessings
Many of which I could see.

Each one lives a life he chooses,
While this should not be ignored,
Just remember each day to be
"Watching the hand of the Lord!"

Acknowledgments

After so many years of preparation for publishing this book, I must first thank our Heavenly Father for the gift of my husband, Phil, for without his input, understanding, and encouragement, I would not have been able to complete it.

To our dear children and their spouses, I am exceedingly thankful for the time and effort you all made in continually reviewing what I had written to make sure the details and outcome of those sections you were directly involved in were accurately recorded.

To the four reviewers of this writing, I am so appreciative of your time and endurance to get through it all and complete your comments in short order when asked to do it.

With special thanks to Pastor Emeritus Daniel Fleischer, who as our pastor for twenty years, was also deeply involved with keeping us in the Word. Your continual writing has been an inspiration to me to get it done!

To Debra Mayhew, with whom I've worked throughout her time as editor of *The Branches* magazine, a special thanks for encouraging me to continue in my writing, whether with my poetry or with this endeavor. I so appreciated all your input.

To Sue Anne Kirkham, a congregational friend for many years both before and after she moved to Texas and back again, and an accomplished writer in her own right, your input from a layman's viewpoint is especially meaningful to me.

To Pastor Emeritus John Schierenbeck, a lifelong
friend, a sincere thank-you for all of your understanding
and spiritual insight in what I was trying to do in this book.

A personal thank you to Tim Schaser, the graphic artist who designed the cover of this book, working diligently to incorporate the elements, colors, and total design. You did this not only through several concepts for me to work with over several weeks, but also while you and your wife, Christina, were being blessed with a new son. Such dedication to your work has been a blessing to the publication of my first book. Thank you, Tim.

My sincere thanks go to Pastor Norman Greve who took the time out of his busy ministerial life to proofread my entire manuscript. I thank our Lord for all your efforts in accomplishing this task for me as you also continue to preach His Word faithfully.

To Sarah Olmanson, an accomplished publishing expert, for the layout of this entire book. I am humbled by your extensive work and willing spirit. I thank you from the bottom of a very grateful heart.

And from a mother's heart, I could not be more blessed by my daughter, Tina, for her years of encouragement and help in getting this book to completion. You have always been there urging me on to *get it done*. At the same time, you have been instrumental through your years in the publishing business to complete it in a correct form and manner. Without that input, I would still be struggling to get it done!

Most of all, I thank my God—Father, Son, and Holy Spirit, Trinity in unity—for the blessings of placing my soul in the hands of His children, my parents, who raised me. He had a plan for each of us and gave me the blessing of watching His plan work in my life. *To God be the glory!*

Selected family members highlighted

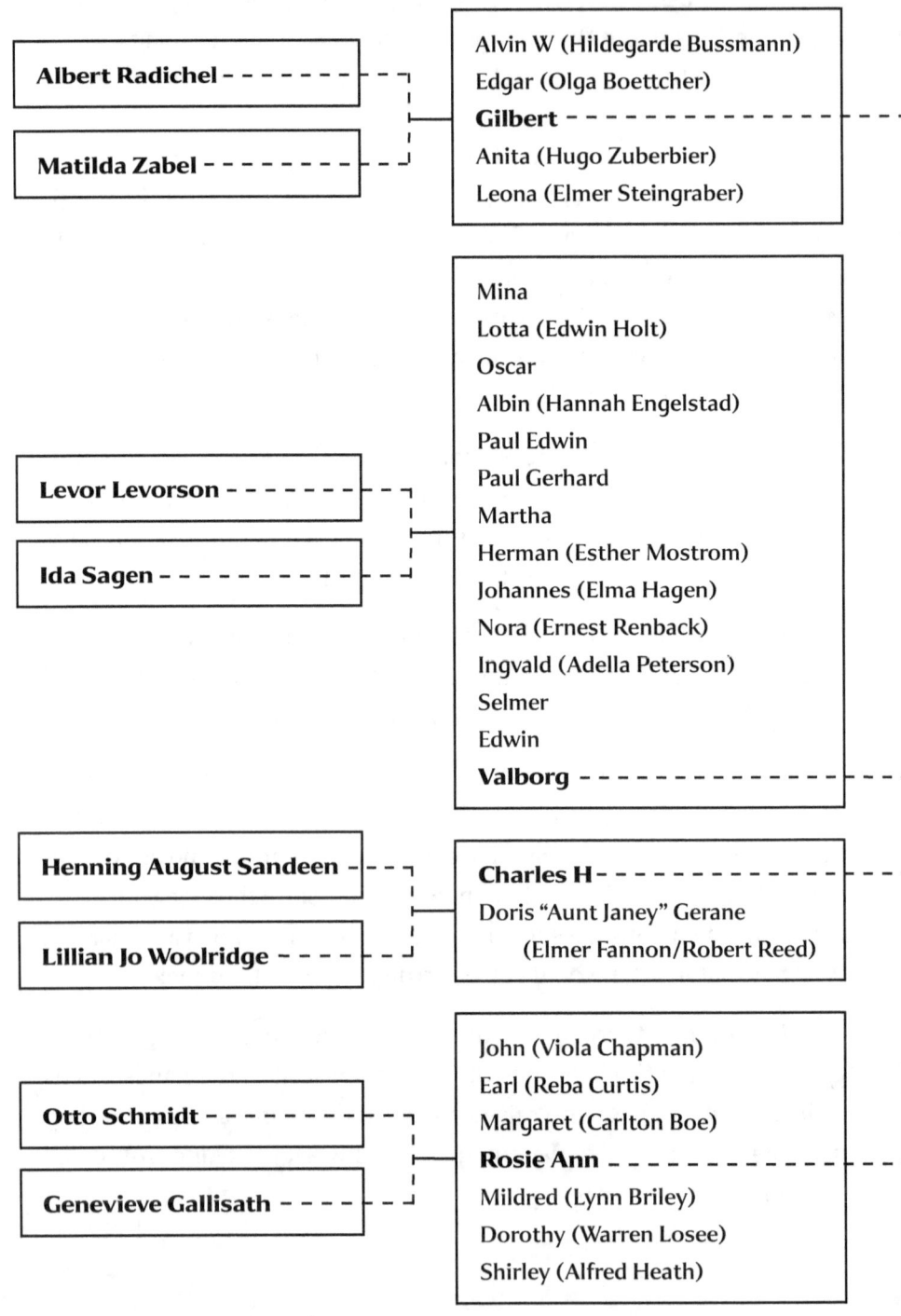

Albert Radichel - - - - - -

Matilda Zabel - - - - - - -

Alvin W (Hildegarde Bussmann)
Edgar (Olga Boettcher)
Gilbert - - - - - - - - - - -
Anita (Hugo Zuberbier)
Leona (Elmer Steingraber)

Levor Levorson - - - - - - -

Ida Sagen - - - - - - - - -

Mina
Lotta (Edwin Holt)
Oscar
Albin (Hannah Engelstad)
Paul Edwin
Paul Gerhard
Martha
Herman (Esther Mostrom)
Johannes (Elma Hagen)
Nora (Ernest Renback)
Ingvald (Adella Peterson)
Selmer
Edwin
Valborg - - - - - - - - - - -

Henning August Sandeen -

Lillian Jo Woolridge - - - -

Charles H - - - - - - - - - -
Doris "Aunt Janey" Gerane
(Elmer Fannon/Robert Reed)

Otto Schmidt - - - - - - -

Genevieve Gallisath - - - -

John (Viola Chapman)
Earl (Reba Curtis)
Margaret (Carlton Boe)
Rosie Ann - - - - - - - -
Mildred (Lynn Briley)
Dorothy (Warren Losee)
Shirley (Alfred Heath)

in *Watching the Hand of the Lord*

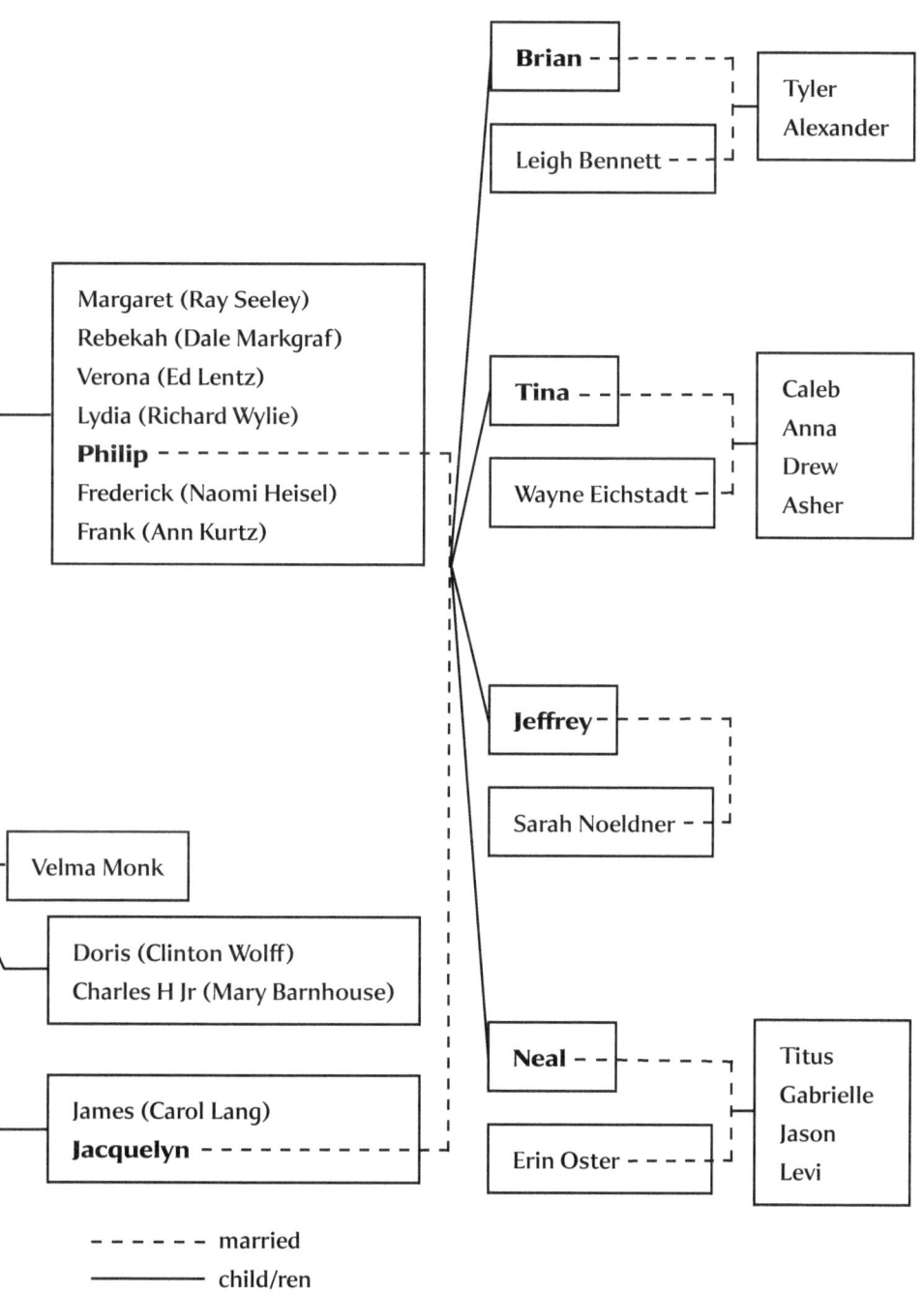

Brian --------
Tyler
Alexander
Leigh Bennett ----

Margaret (Ray Seeley)
Rebekah (Dale Markgraf)
Verona (Ed Lentz)
Lydia (Richard Wylie)
Philip ----------
Frederick (Naomi Heisel)
Frank (Ann Kurtz)

Tina ----------
Caleb
Anna
Drew
Wayne Eichstadt -- Asher

Jeffrey -----
Sarah Noeldner ---

Velma Monk

Doris (Clinton Wolff)
Charles H Jr (Mary Barnhouse)

James (Carol Lang)
Jacquelyn ----------

Neal ----------
Titus
Gabrielle
Jason
Erin Oster ---- Levi

- - - - - - married
————— child/ren

To God be the glory!

www.ingramcontent.com/pod-product-compliance
Lightning Source LLC
Chambersburg PA
CBHW070659130626
46553CB00005B/1772